Max Lucado

Life Lessons *from*

2 Corinthians

Remembering What Matters

Prepared by The Livingstone Corporation

Thomas Nelson
Since 1798

Published in Nashville, Tennessee, by Thomas Nelson. Thomas Nelson is a registered trademark of HarperCollins Christian Publishing, Inc.

Produced with the assistance of the Livingstone Corporation. Project staff include Jake Barton, Joel Bartlett, Andy Culbertson, Mary Horner Collins, Will Reaves, and Rachel Hawkins.

Editor: Len Woods

All Scripture quotations, unless otherwise indicated, are taken from The Holy Bible, New International Version®, NIV®. Copyright © 1973, 1978, 1984, 2011 by Biblica, Inc.™ Used by permission. All rights reserved worldwide.

Scripture quotations marked MSG taken from THE MESSAGE. Copyright © 1993, 1994, 1995, 1996, 2000, 2001, 2002. Used by permission of NavPress. All rights reserved. Represented by Tyndale House Publishers, Inc.

Scripture quotations marked NCV are taken from The Holy Bible, New Century Version®. Copyright © 1987, 1988, 1991 by Thomas Nelson,

Scripture quotations marked NKJV are taken from the New King James Version®. Copyright © 1982 by Thomas Nelson. Used by permission. All rights reserved.

Scripture quotations marked PHILLIPS taken from The New Testament in Modern English, Revised Edition. Copyright © J.B. Phillips 1958, 1960, 1972. Used by permission of Macmillan Publishing Co., Inc.

Material for the "Inspiration" sections taken from the following books:

3:16—The Numbers of Hope. Copyright © 2007 by Max Lucado. Thomas Nelson, a registered trademark of HarperCollins Christian Publishing, Inc., Nashville, Tennessee.

Come Thirsty. Copyright © 2004 by Max Lucado. Thomas Nelson, a registered trademark of HarperCollins Christian Publishing, Inc., Nashville, Tennessee.

Cure for the Common Life. Copyright © 2005 by Max Lucado. Thomas Nelson, a registered trademark of HarperCollins Christian Publishing, Inc., Nashville, Tennessee.

A Gentle Thunder. Copyright © 1995 by Max Lucado. Thomas Nelson, a registered trademark of HarperCollins Christian Publishing, Inc., Nashville, Tennessee.

Grace. Copyright © 2012 by Max Lucado. Thomas Nelson, a registered trademark of HarperCollins Christian Publishing, Inc., Nashville, Tennessee.

In the Grip of Grace. Copyright © 1996 by Max Lucado. Thomas Nelson, a registered trademark of HarperCollins Christian Publishing, Inc., Nashville, Tennessee.

It's Not About Me. Copyright © 2004 by Max Lucado. Thomas Nelson, a registered trademark of HarperCollins Christian Publishing, Inc., Nashville, Tennessee.

Just Like Jesus. Copyright © 1998 by Max Lucado. Thomas Nelson, a registered trademark of HarperCollins Christian Publishing, Inc., Nashville, Tennessee.

Traveling Light. Copyright © 2001 by Max Lucado. Thomas Nelson, a registered trademark of HarperCollins Christian Publishing, Inc., Nashville, Tennessee.

When God Whispers Your Name. Copyright © 1994, 1999 by Max Lucado. Thomas Nelson, a registered trademark of HarperCollins Christian Publishing, Inc., Nashville, Tennessee.

You'll Get Through This. Copyright © 2013 by Max Lucado. Thomas Nelson, a registered trademark of HarperCollins Christian Publishing, Inc., Nashville, Tennessee.

Thomas Nelson titles may be purchased in bulk for educational, business, fundraising, or sales promotional use. For information, please e-mail SpecialMarkets@ThomasNelson.com.

ISBN 978-0-310-08644-4

First Printing May 2018 / Printed in the United States of America

CONTENTS

HOW TO STUDY THE BIBLE

The Bible is a peculiar book. Words crafted in another language. Deeds done in a distant era. Events recorded in a far-off land. Counsel offered to a foreign people. It is a peculiar book.

It's surprising that anyone reads it. It's too old. Some of its writings date back 5,000 years. It's too bizarre. The book speaks of incredible floods, fires, earthquakes, and people with supernatural abilities. It's too radical. The Bible calls for undying devotion to a carpenter who called himself God's Son.

Logic says this book shouldn't survive. Too old, too bizarre, too radical.

The Bible has been banned, burned, scoffed, and ridiculed. Scholars have mocked it as foolish. Kings have branded it as illegal. A thousand times over the grave has been dug and the dirge has begun, but somehow the Bible never stays in the grave. Not only has it survived, but it has also thrived. It is the single most popular book in all of history. It has been the bestselling book in the world for years!

There is no way on earth to explain it. Which perhaps is the only explanation. For the Bible's durability is not found on *earth* but in *heaven*. The millions who have tested its claims and claimed its promises know there is but one answer: the Bible is God's book and God's voice.

As you read it, you would be wise to give some thought to two questions: *What is the purpose of the Bible?* and *How do I study the Bible?* Time spent reflecting on these two issues will greatly enhance your Bible study.

What is the purpose of the Bible?

Let the Bible itself answer that question: *"From infancy you have known the Holy Scriptures, which are able to make you wise for salvation through faith in Christ Jesus"* (2 Timothy 3:15).

The purpose of the Bible? Salvation. God's highest passion is to get his children home. His book, the Bible, describes his plan of salvation. The purpose of the Bible is to proclaim God's plan and passion to save his children.

This is the reason why this book has endured through the centuries. It dares to tackle the toughest questions about life: *Where do I go after I die? Is there a God? What do I do with my fears?* The Bible is the treasure map that leads to God's highest treasure—eternal life.

But how do you study the Bible? Countless copies of Scripture sit unread on bookshelves and nightstands simply because people don't know how to read it. What can you do to make the Bible real in your life?

The clearest answer is found in the words of Jesus: *"Ask and it will be given to you; seek and you will find; knock and the door will be opened to you"* (Matthew 7:7).

The first step in understanding the Bible is asking God to help you. You should read it prayerfully. If anyone understands God's Word, it is because of God and not the reader.

"The Advocate, the Holy Spirit, whom the Father will send in my name, will teach you all things and will remind you of everything I have said to you" (John 14:26).

Before reading the Bible, pray and invite God to speak to you. Don't go to Scripture looking for your idea, but go searching for his.

Not only should you read the Bible prayerfully, but you should also read it carefully. *"Seek and you will find"* is the pledge. The Bible is not a newspaper to be skimmed but rather a mine to be quarried. *"If you look for it as for silver and search for it as for hidden treasure, then you will understand the fear of the LORD and find the knowledge of God"* (Proverbs 2:4–5).

Any worthy find requires effort. The Bible is no exception. To understand the Bible, you don't have to be brilliant, but you must be willing to roll up your sleeves and search.

"Do your best to present yourself to God as one approved, a worker who does not need to be ashamed and who correctly handles the word of truth" (2 Timothy 2:15).

Here's a practical point. Study the Bible a bit at a time. Hunger is not satisfied by eating twenty-one meals in one sitting once a week. The body needs a steady diet to remain strong. So does the soul. When God sent food to his people in the wilderness, he didn't provide loaves already made. Instead, he sent them manna in the shape of *"thin flakes like frost on the ground"* (Exodus 16:14).

God gave manna in limited portions.

God sends spiritual food the same way. He opens the heavens with just enough nutrients for today's hunger. He provides *"a rule for this, a rule for that; a little here, a little there"* (Isaiah 28:10).

Don't be discouraged if your reading reaps a small harvest. Some days a lesser portion is all that is needed. What is important is to search every day for that day's message. A steady diet of God's Word over a lifetime builds a healthy soul and mind.

It's much like the little girl who returned from her first day at school feeling a bit dejected. Her mom asked, "Did you learn anything?"

"Apparently not enough," the girl responded. "I have to go back tomorrow, and the next day, and the next . . ."

Such is the case with learning. And such is the case with Bible study. Understanding comes little by little over a lifetime.

There is a third step in understanding the Bible. After the asking and seeking comes the knocking. After you ask and search, *"knock and the door will be opened to you"* (Matthew 7:7).

To knock is to stand at God's door. To make yourself available. To climb the steps, cross the porch, stand at the doorway, and volunteer. Knocking goes beyond the realm of thinking and into the realm of acting.

To knock is to ask, *What can I do? How can I obey? Where can I go?*

It's one thing to know what to do. It's another to do it. But for those who do it—those who choose to obey—a special reward awaits them.

"Whoever looks intently into the perfect law that gives freedom, and continues in it—not forgetting what they have heard, but doing it—they will be blessed in what they do" (James 1:25).

What a promise. Blessings come to those who do what they read in God's Word! It's the same with medicine. If you only read the label but ignore the pills, it won't help. It's the same with food. If you only read the recipe but never cook, you won't be fed. And it's the same with the Bible. If you only read the words but never obey, you'll never know the joy God has promised.

Ask. Search. Knock. Simple, isn't it? So why don't you give it a try? If you do, you'll see why the Bible is the most remarkable book in history.

At a school in a small village, there was one girl who came early. She helped the teacher prepare the room for the day. The same girl would stay late—cleaning the board and dusting the erasers. During class, she was attentive. She sat close to the teacher, absorbing the lessons.

One day when the other children were unruly and inattentive, the teacher used the girl as an example. "Why can't you be like her? She listens. She works. She comes early. She stays late."

"It isn't fair to ask us to be like her," a boy blurted out from the rear of the room. "Why?" asked the teacher.

The boy was uncomfortable, wishing he hadn't spoken. "She has an advantage," he shrugged. "She is an orphan," he almost whispered.

The boy was right. The girl had an advantage. An advantage of knowing that school, as tedious as it was, was better than the orphanage. Since she knew that, she appreciated what the others took for granted.

We, too, were orphans. Alone.

No name. No future. No hope.

Were it not for our adoption as his children, we would have no place to belong. We sometimes forget that.

The Corinthians forgot.

They had grown puffy in their achievements and divisive in their fellowship. They argued over the correct leader, the greater gifts. They rebelled against Paul's leadership. They were indifferent to sin and insensitive in worship.

Paul defends his ministry and admonishes the Christians to remember to whom they belong. "Examine yourselves," Paul says (2 Corinthians 13:5). Paul's words are clear. "If anyone is in Christ, the new creation has come: The old has gone, the new is here!" (5:17).

Good reminder.

Not just for them but for us as well. For if we forget, we, too, will be like the students who did just enough to pass the grade and never enough to show their thanks.

AUTHOR AND DATE

Paul, who persecuted the early church before his life was radically altered by meeting the risen Jesus on the road to Damascus (see Acts 9:1–31). Paul first arrived in Corinth after a disappointing visit to Athens, where he was unable to establish a church (see 17:16–34). There he met two Jewish believers and fellow tentmakers, Priscilla and Aquila, and together they formed a church. Paul's success in Corinth led to both Jews and Gentiles, from all backgrounds and walks of life, accepting Christ and joining the community. In turn, this would lead to certain challenges among the believers as they sought to separate from their past and walk in their new lives in Christ, which Paul would address in a series of letters. It is likely Paul wrote 2 Corinthians c. AD 56, a year after writing 1 Corinthians, from Macedonia (like Philippi, Thessalonica, or Berea). Titus, his fellow minister to the congregation, delivered it.

SITUATION

After Paul wrote his first epistle to the Corinthians, reports began to arrive from Titus that in his absence, teachers from Judea had arrived and were challenging his integrity and authority as an apostle. In response, Paul made a quick trip to Corinth to correct the situation, but the visit proved to be painful and unproductive. When Paul returned to Ephesus, he wrote the Corinthians a "severe" letter, but then was forced to flee when the silversmiths in the city caused a riot (see Acts 19:23–41). Paul eventually relocated to Macedonia, where, to his relief, Titus reported the Corinthians had responded favorably to his severe letter. This report prompted Paul to write was is now known as 2 Corinthians 1–9. Meanwhile, the teachers from Judea continued to undermine Paul's authority in the church, prompting Paul to follow up his letter with what is now known as 2 Corinthians 10–13.

KEY THEMES

- Faith in Christ brings new life.
- God's people should give of their income to support God's work in the world.
- God can work through us no matter who we are.

KEY VERSES

Therefore, if anyone is in Christ, he is a new creation; old things have passed away; behold, all things have become new (2 Corinthians 5:17 NKJV).

CONTENTS

LESSON ONE

SUFFERING

*Blessed be the God and Father of our Lord Jesus Christ . . .
who comforts us in all our tribulation, that we may
be able to comfort those who are in any trouble.*
2 CORINTHIANS 1:3–4 NKJV

REFLECTION

Life is full of ups and downs. We can be cruising along, with everything going well—and then, suddenly, the wheels go flying off. We find ourselves in the proverbial ditch, asking ourselves, "What just happened?" Which end of the spectrum best describes your life right now?

_____

_____

_____

_____

_____

_____

SITUATION

In the book of Acts, we read that after a man named Demetrius and his fellow silversmiths caused a riot in Ephesus, "Paul sent for the disciples and, after encouraging them, said goodbye and set out for Macedonia" (20:1). During this time, Paul underwent some form of life-or-death experience. The Corinthians had evidently heard about his crises, for Paul does feel the need to mention the specifics of his ordeals. He does, however, take the time to thank the Corinthians for their prayers and reassure them that God, in his grace, had delivered him from those trials.

OBSERVATION

Read 2 Corinthians 1:1–11 from the New International Version or the New King James Version.

New International Version
¹ Paul, an apostle of Christ Jesus by the will of God, and Timothy our brother,

To the church of God in Corinth, together with all his holy people throughout Achaia:

2 Grace and peace to you from God our Father and the Lord Jesus Christ.

3 Praise be to the God and Father of our Lord Jesus Christ, the Father of compassion and the God of all comfort, 4 who comforts us in all our troubles, so that we can comfort those in any trouble with the comfort we ourselves receive from God. 5 For just as we share abundantly in the sufferings of Christ, so also our comfort abounds through Christ. 6 If we are distressed, it is for your comfort and salvation; if we are comforted, it is for your comfort, which produces in you patient endurance of the same sufferings we suffer. 7 And our hope for you is firm, because we know that just as you share in our sufferings, so also you share in our comfort.

8 We do not want you to be uninformed, brothers and sisters, about the troubles we experienced in the province of Asia. We were under great pressure, far beyond our ability to endure, so that we despaired of life itself. 9 Indeed, we felt we had received the sentence of death. But this happened that we might not rely on ourselves but on God, who raises the dead. 10 He has delivered us from such a deadly peril, and he will deliver us again. On him we have set our hope that he will continue to deliver us, 11 as you help us by your prayers. Then many will give thanks on our behalf for the gracious favor granted us in answer to the prayers of many.

New King James Version

1 Paul, an apostle of Jesus Christ by the will of God, and Timothy our brother,

To the church of God which is at Corinth, with all the saints who are in all Achaia:

2 Grace to you and peace from God our Father and the Lord Jesus Christ.

3 Blessed be the God and Father of our Lord Jesus Christ, the Father of mercies and God of all comfort, 4 who comforts us in all our tribulation, that we may be able to comfort those who are in any trouble, with

the comfort with which we ourselves are comforted by God. ⁵ For as the sufferings of Christ abound in us, so our consolation also abounds through Christ. ⁶ Now if we are afflicted, it is for your consolation and salvation, which is effective for enduring the same sufferings which we also suffer. Or if we are comforted, it is for your consolation and salvation. ⁷ And our hope for you is steadfast, because we know that as you are partakers of the sufferings, so also you will partake of the consolation.

⁸ For we do not want you to be ignorant, brethren, of our trouble which came to us in Asia: that we were burdened beyond measure, above strength, so that we despaired even of life. ⁹ Yes, we had the sentence of death in ourselves, that we should not trust in ourselves but in God who raises the dead, ¹⁰ who delivered us from so great a death, and does deliver us; in whom we trust that He will still deliver us, ¹¹ you also helping together in prayer for us, that thanks may be given by many persons on our behalf for the gift granted to us through many.

EXPLORATION

1. Why is it significant, based on the information you have read about the situation in Corinth, that Paul describes himself as "an apostle of Christ Jesus by the will of God" (verse 1)?

_____

_____

_____

_____

2. What do you think Paul means when he writes to the Corinthians, "If we are distressed, it is for your comfort and salvation" (verse 6)?

_____

_____

_____

_____

3. How does Paul describe God in this passage?

_____

_____

_____

_____

4. How would you explain the difference between *hope* and *comfort*?

_____

_____

_____

_____

5. Paul provides a window into his emotional state during the worst of these recent trials. What are some of the key words and phrases he uses to describe his ordeals?

_____

_____

_____

_____

6. What is Paul's perspective on these trials that he has faced? Why he does he believe that he was allowed to undergo them?

_____

_____

_____

_____

INSPIRATION

You'll get through this. You fear you won't. We all do. We fear that the depression will never lift, the yelling will never stop, the pain will never leave. Here in the pits . . . we wonder, *Will this gray sky ever brighten?*

This load ever lighten? We feel stuck, trapped, locked in. Predestined for failure. *Will we ever exit this pit?*

Yes! Deliverance is to the Bible what jazz music is to Mardi Gras: bold, brassy, and everywhere.

Out of the lions' den for Daniel, the prison for Peter, the whale's belly for Jonah, Goliath's shadow for David, the storm for the disciples, disease for the lepers, doubt for Thomas, the grave for Lazarus, and the shackles for Paul. God gets us through stuff. *Through* the Red Sea onto dry ground (see Exodus 14:22), *through* the wilderness (see Deuteronomy 29:5), *through* the valley of the shadow of death (see Psalm 23:4), and *through* the deep sea (see 77:19).

Through is a favorite word of God's: "When you pass *through* the waters, I will be with you; and when you pass through the rivers, they will not sweep over you. When you walk through the fire, you will not be burned; the flames will not set you ablaze" (Isaiah 43:2).

It won't be painless. Have you wept your final tear or received your last round of chemotherapy? Not necessarily. Will your unhappy marriage become happy in a heartbeat? Not likely. Are you exempt from any trip to the cemetery? Does God guarantee the absence of struggle and the abundance of strength? Not in this life. But he does pledge to reweave your pain for a higher purpose.

It won't be quick. . . . Sometimes God takes his time: 120 years to prepare Noah for the flood, eighty years to prepare Moses for his work. God called young David to be king but returned him to the sheep pasture. He called Paul to be an apostle and then isolated him in Arabia for perhaps three years. Jesus was on the earth for three decades before he built anything more than a kitchen table. How long will God take with you? He may take his time. His history is redeemed not in minutes but in lifetimes.

But God will use your mess for good. We see a perfect mess; God sees a perfect chance to train, test, and teach us. . . . We see Satan's tricks and ploys. God sees Satan tripped and foiled. (From *You'll Get Through This* by Max Lucado.)

REACTION

7. What evidence has God provided in the Bible that he delivers his children from trials?

_____

_____

_____

_____

_____

8. Think back over your life to the hardest trials and most excruciating times of suffering. What got you _through_ those events?

_____

_____

_____

_____

_____

9. What are some of the ways that God brings comfort to his hurting children?

_____

_____

_____

_____

_____

10. Many people in the midst of difficulty become negative and resort to incessant complaining. Not Paul. How do you think he maintained his hopeful outlook?

_____

_____

_____

_____

11. How do you respond to the statement that God will get you through a trial—but it won't necessarily be painless or quick?

_____

_____

_____

12. How have you, like Paul, looked back on the trials you've faced and seen how God ultimately used the situation for good?

_____

_____

_____

LIFE LESSONS

A renowned psychiatrist was once asked how to overcome depression. His advice? "Get dressed, lock your house, go find someone who is in need, and serve that person." In other words, get the focus off yourself and look for ways to help others. This others-centered mindset is to be the hallmark of every Christian's life. Jesus constantly lived to serve others, and the apostle Paul did likewise. In a situation where lesser men would have decided to throw a major "pity party," licking their wounds and lamenting their woeful condition, Paul turned to God for comfort. He then picked up a pen and determined to write a letter that would help the Corinthians think and live in ways that honored God.

DEVOTION

Thank you, God, for being our merciful Father and the source of ultimate comfort. You are so faithful and good! Teach us the habit of looking to you to meet all our needs. Show us how to draw on your infinite resources so we might be a source of compassion to others who hurt.

JOURNALING

What are some practical ways that you can start to change your attitude about your trials?

FOR FURTHER READING

To complete the book of 2 Corinthians during this twelve-part study, read 2 Corinthians 1:1–11. For more Bible passages on looking to God for comfort in suffering, read Psalm 23:1–4; 119:50–52; John 14:16–17; Philippians 2:1–2; and James 1:3–12.

LESSON TWO

PLANNING AND INTEGRITY

*Now this is our boast: Our conscience testifies that we have
conducted ourselves in the world, and especially in our
relations with you, with integrity and godly sincerity.*
2 Corinthians 1:12

REFLECTION

Perhaps you've heard the old phrase, "The best laid plans often go astray." Even the most carefully considered and thought-out agendas can go awry at times! What was a recent situation in your life where your plans did not work out as you intended? How did you respond?

_____

_____

_____

_____

_____

_____

_____

_____

_____

_____

_____

_____

_____

SITUATION

As previously mentioned, one of Paul's aims in writing this letter to the Corinthians was to defend his credibility and his authority as an apostle. It seems that in his absence, individuals from Judea (see 2 Corinthians 11:21–22) had arrived and questioned his integrity, charging, among other things, that Paul was fickle because he did not keep his commitment to visit them. In response, Paul explains the reason for his change in plans and why it was done for _their_ benefit—not for any personal gain or self-interests on his part.

OBSERVATION

Read 2 Corinthians 1:12–2:4 from the New International
Version or the New King James Version.

New International Version

1:12 Now this is our boast: Our conscience testifies that we have conducted ourselves in the world, and especially in our relations with you, with integrity and godly sincerity. We have done so, relying not on worldly wisdom but on God's grace. 13 For we do not write you anything you cannot read or understand. And I hope that, 14 as you have understood us in part, you will come to understand fully that you can boast of us just as we will boast of you in the day of the Lord Jesus.

15 Because I was confident of this, I wanted to visit you first so that you might benefit twice. 16 I wanted to visit you on my way to Macedonia and to come back to you from Macedonia, and then to have you send me on my way to Judea. 17 Was I fickle when I intended to do this? Or do I make my plans in a worldly manner so that in the same breath I say both "Yes, yes" and "No, no"?

18 But as surely as God is faithful, our message to you is not "Yes" and "No." 19 For the Son of God, Jesus Christ, who was preached among you by us—by me and Silas and Timothy—was not "Yes" and "No," but in him it has always been "Yes." 20 For no matter how many promises God has made, they are "Yes" in Christ. And so through him the "Amen" is spoken by us to the glory of God. 21 Now it is God who makes both us and you stand firm in Christ. He anointed us, 22 set his seal of ownership on us, and put his Spirit in our hearts as a deposit, guaranteeing what is to come.

23 I call God as my witness—and I stake my life on it—that it was in order to spare you that I did not return to Corinth. 24 Not that we lord it over your faith, but we work with you for your joy, because it is by faith you stand firm. 2:1 So I made up my mind that I would not make another painful visit to you. 2 For if I grieve you, who is left to make me glad but you whom I have grieved? 3 I wrote as I did, so that when I came I would not be

distressed by those who should have made me rejoice. I had confidence in all of you, that you would all share my joy. 4 For I wrote you out of great distress and anguish of heart and with many tears, not to grieve you but to let you know the depth of my love for you.

NEW KING JAMES VERSION

1:12 For our boasting is this: the testimony of our conscience that we conducted ourselves in the world in simplicity and godly sincerity, not with fleshly wisdom but by the grace of God, and more abundantly toward you. 13 For we are not writing any other things to you than what you read or understand. Now I trust you will understand, even to the end 14 (as also you have understood us in part), that we are your boast as you also are ours, in the day of the Lord Jesus.

15 And in this confidence I intended to come to you before, that you might have a second benefit— 16 to pass by way of you to Macedonia, to come again from Macedonia to you, and be helped by you on my way to Judea. 17 Therefore, when I was planning this, did I do it lightly? Or the things I plan, do I plan according to the flesh, that with me there should be Yes, Yes, and No, No? 18 But as God is faithful, our word to you was not Yes and No. 19 For the Son of God, Jesus Christ, who was preached among you by us—by me, Silvanus, and Timothy—was not Yes and No, but in Him was Yes. 20 For all the promises of God in Him are Yes, and in Him Amen, to the glory of God through us. 21 Now He who establishes us with you in Christ and has anointed us is God, 22 who also has sealed us and given us the Spirit in our hearts as a guarantee.

23 Moreover I call God as witness against my soul, that to spare you I came no more to Corinth. 24 Not that we have dominion over your faith, but are fellow workers for your joy; for by faith you stand.

2:1 But I determined this within myself, that I would not come again to you in sorrow. 2 For if I make you sorrowful, then who is he who makes me glad but the one who is made sorrowful by me?

3 And I wrote this very thing to you, lest, when I came, I should have sorrow over those from whom I ought to have joy, having confidence in

you all that my joy is the joy of you all. [4] For out of much affliction and anguish of heart I wrote to you, with many tears, not that you should be grieved, but that you might know the love which I have so abundantly for you.

EXPLORATION

1. What situation gave the individuals from Judea cause to level charges against Paul?

_____

_____

_____

_____

2. What does Paul claim in this passage about his true motives?

_____

_____

_____

_____

3. How does Paul say the believers benefited twice because of his change in plans?

_____

_____

_____

_____

4. How does Paul differentiate between his way of planning and the world's way of planning?

_____

_____

_____

_____

5. What do you think Paul means when he says that his message to the believers was not "yes" and "no"? How does he describe his relationship with them?

_____

_____

_____

_____

6. When are some times in your life that you had to revise your plans for another person's benefit? How did that person react to the change?

_____

_____

_____

INSPIRATION

When David, who was a warrior, minstrel, and ambassador for God, searched for an illustration of God, he remembered his days as a shepherd. He remembered how he lavished attention on the sheep day and night. How he slept with them and watched over them. And the way he cared for the sheep reminded him of the way God cares for us. David rejoiced to say, "The LORD is my shepherd" (Psalm 23:1), and in so doing he proudly implied, "I am his sheep."

Still uncomfortable with being considered a sheep? Will you humor me and take a simple quiz? See if you succeed in self-reliance. Raise your hand if any of the following describe you.

You can control your moods. You're never grumpy or sullen. You can't relate to Jekyll and Hyde. You're always upbeat and upright. Does that describe you? No? Well, let's try another.

You are at peace with everyone. Every relationship as sweet as fudge. Even your old flames speak highly of you. Love all and are loved by all. Is that you? If not, how about this description?

You have no fears. Call you the Teflon toughie. Wall Street plummets—no problem. Heart condition discovered—yawn. World War III starts—what's for dinner?

Does this describe you? *You need no forgiveness.* Never made a mistake. As square as a game of checkers. As clean as grandma's kitchen. Never cheated, never lied, never lied about cheating. Is that you? No?

Let's evaluate this. You can't control your moods. A few of your relationships are shaky. You have fears and faults. Hmmm. Do you really want to hang on to your chest of self-reliance? Sounds to me as if you could use a shepherd. (From *Traveling Light* by Max Lucado.)

REACTION

7. The "job description" of a sheep is to go wherever the shepherd guides it. Why is it so hard for Christians to let go of their agendas and follow Christ?

---

8. How do you try to conduct yourself with "integrity and godly sincerity" (2 Corinthians 1:12)?

---

9. When you sense God leading you in a different direction than you had planned, how do you typically respond?

---

10. How does a Christian develop the ability to follow wherever the Holy Spirit is leading?

_____

_____

_____

_____

11. How do you respond when your actions are misunderstood, you are unfairly accused, or your character is called into question?

_____

_____

_____

_____

12. Why do you think Paul had such a deep love and relentless concern for a church that had caused him so much grief?

_____

_____

_____

_____

LIFE LESSONS

One thing we can count on for sure is the unpredictability of life. If we commit to follow Christ, the Good Shepherd, we should expect the unexpected. Sometimes divinely allowed or orchestrated events will block our path. God's Spirit will suddenly nudge us down a different course. In some situations, our "new" plans or direction may be viewed as foolish by others. Our wisdom and character, perhaps even our sanity, will be called into question. Our calling is not to do what is wise in the world's eyes, nor is it to take the popular course of action. Rather than wrangle with God, we are to submit to his leading, however "odd" it may seem.

DEVOTION

Lord, we want to become more sensitive to your leading and better able to discern your voice. We want to devote our days to doing your will, not pursuing our own agendas. No matter what it means, give us the courage to go everywhere you direct and do everything you instruct.

JOURNALING

What are your specific fears of turning over your personal calendar to God and saying, "Not my will, but your will be done"?

FOR FURTHER READING

To complete the book of 2 Corinthians during this twelve-part study, read 2 Corinthians 1:12–2:13. For more Bible passages on planning, read Psalm 33:10–11; Proverbs 15:22; 16:3, 9; 19:21; Isaiah 29:15; and James 4:13–14.

LESSON THREE

GOD'S NEW AGREEMENT

*But we all, with unveiled face, beholding as
in a mirror the glory of the Lord, are being
transformed into the same image from glory
to glory, just as by the Spirit of the Lord.*
2 CORINTHIANS 3:18 NKJV

REFLECTION

Household standards. Civic ordinances. Congressional legislation. Life is full of rules and regulations. What were some of the hard-and-fast requirements you were forced to live by growing up? What were the consequences if you violated those rules?

SITUATION

In the next section of Paul's letter, he turns his attention to the teachers from Judea who have criticized him and his work among the Corinthians. These individuals were stating that believers in Christ had to adopt certain Jewish practices and adhere to the Law of Moses in order to earn God's approval. Paul responds to this claim by discussing the limits of the old covenant and why the new life found in Christ brings freedom and removes the barrier between us and God.

OBSERVATION

Read 2 Corinthians 3:4–18 from the New International Version or the New King James Version.

New International Version

⁴ Such confidence we have through Christ before God. ⁵ Not that we are competent in ourselves to claim anything for ourselves, but our competence comes from God. ⁶ He has made us competent as ministers of a

new covenant—not of the letter but of the Spirit; for the letter kills, but the Spirit gives life.

[7] Now if the ministry that brought death, which was engraved in letters on stone, came with glory, so that the Israelites could not look steadily at the face of Moses because of its glory, transitory though it was, [8] will not the ministry of the Spirit be even more glorious? [9] If the ministry that brought condemnation was glorious, how much more glorious is the ministry that brings righteousness! [10] For what was glorious has no glory now in comparison with the surpassing glory. [11] And if what was transitory came with glory, how much greater is the glory of that which lasts!

[12] Therefore, since we have such a hope, we are very bold. [13] We are not like Moses, who would put a veil over his face to prevent the Israelites from seeing the end of what was passing away. [14] But their minds were made dull, for to this day the same veil remains when the old covenant is read. It has not been removed, because only in Christ is it taken away.[15] Even to this day when Moses is read, a veil covers their hearts. [16] But whenever anyone turns to the Lord, the veil is taken away. [17] Now the Lord is the Spirit, and where the Spirit of the Lord is, there is freedom. [18] And we all, who with unveiled faces contemplate the Lord's glory, are being transformed into his image with ever-increasing glory, which comes from the Lord, who is the Spirit.

New King James Version

[4] And we have such trust through Christ toward God. [5] Not that we are sufficient of ourselves to think of anything as being from ourselves, but our sufficiency is from God, [6] who also made us sufficient as ministers of the new covenant, not of the letter but of the Spirit; for the letter kills, but the Spirit gives life.

[7] But if the ministry of death, written and engraved on stones, was glorious, so that the children of Israel could not look steadily at the face of Moses because of the glory of his countenance, which glory was passing away, [8] how will the ministry of the Spirit not be more glorious? [9] For if the ministry of condemnation had glory, the ministry of righteousness

exceeds much more in glory. [10] For even what was made glorious had no glory in this respect, because of the glory that excels. [11] For if what is passing away was glorious, what remains is much more glorious.

[12] Therefore, since we have such hope, we use great boldness of speech— [13] unlike Moses, who put a veil over his face so that the children of Israel could not look steadily at the end of what was passing away. [14] But their minds were blinded. For until this day the same veil remains unlifted in the reading of the Old Testament, because the veil is taken away in Christ. [15] But even to this day, when Moses is read, a veil lies on their heart. [16] Nevertheless when one turns to the Lord, the veil is taken away. [17] Now the Lord is the Spirit; and where the Spirit of the Lord is, there is liberty. [18] But we all, with unveiled face, beholding as in a mirror the glory of the Lord, are being transformed into the same image from glory to glory, just as by the Spirit of the Lord.

EXPLORATION

1. How would you explain the difference between the old covenant (divine rules written on tablets of stone) and the new covenant under Christ?

_____

_____

_____

2. What does Paul mean when he says "the letter kills, but the Spirit gives life" (verse 6)?

_____

_____

_____

3. Where does Paul say we can find the power to live as God expects?

_____

_____

_____

4. What does Paul reveal about the effect of God's law? What did it bring to God's people?

_____

_____

_____

5. Paul compares the inferior glory of the old covenant with the surpassing glory of God's new agreement. What exactly _is_ glory?

_____

_____

_____

6. How would you describe the difference between external pressure to do something and the internal desire to accomplish it?

_____

_____

_____

INSPIRATION

"For God so loved the world that he gave his one and only Son, that whoever believes in him shall not perish but have eternal life" (John 3:16).

Can we really believe these words? Can we trust that "whoever believes in Christ shall not perish"? Jesus' invitation seems too simple. We gravitate to other verbs. _Work_ has a better ring to it. "Whoever works for him will be saved." _Satisfy_ fits nicely. "Whoever satisfies him will be saved." But _believe_? Shouldn't I do more?

This seems to be the struggle of Nicodemus. It was his conversation with Christ, remember, that set the stage for John 3:16. Jesus' "you must be born again" command struck him as odd. The baby takes a passive role in the birthing process. The infant allows the parent to do the work.

Salvation is equally simple. God works and we trust. Such a thought troubles Nicodemus. There must be more.

Jesus comforts the visiting professor with an account from the Torah, Nicodemus's favorite book. "Just as Moses lifted up the snake in the wilderness, so the Son of Man must be lifted up, that everyone who believes may have eternal life in him" (John 3:14–15). . . .

This passage was a solemn prophecy. And it was also a simple promise. Snake-bit Israelites found healing by looking at the pole. Sinners will find healing by looking to Christ. "Everyone who believes may have eternal life in him."

The simplicity troubles many people. We expect a more complicated cure, a more elaborate treatment. Moses and his followers might have expected more as well. Manufacture an ointment. Invent a therapeutic lotion. Treat one another. Or at least fight back. Break out the sticks and stones and attack the snakes.

We, too, expect a more proactive assignment, to have to conjure up a remedy for our sin. Some mercy seekers have donned hair shirts, climbed cathedral steps on their knees, or traversed hot rocks on bare feet.

Others of us have written our own Bible verse: "God helps those who help themselves." We'll fix ourselves, thank you. We'll make up for our mistakes with contributions, our guilt with busyness. We'll overcome failures with hard work. We'll find salvation the old-fashioned way: we'll earn it.

Christ, in contrast, says to us, "Your part is to trust. Trust me to do what you can't" (From *3:16: The Numbers of Hope* by Max Lucado.)

REACTION

7. In what ways is the Christian explanation of salvation counter-intuitive to our human nature?

_____

_____

_____

_____

8. Why do you think people have trouble accepting there is nothing they can do to *earn* their salvation—that it is a completely free gift of God?

_____

_____

_____

9. What are some things you have done in the past out of a sense of guilt or need to feel that you are "worthy" enough for God's approval?

_____

_____

_____

10. How does accepting Christ as your Savior lead to this kind of "veil" being taken away from your heart? What new understanding did you gain after coming to Christ?

_____

_____

_____

11. What other ways have you seen God working in your life since you put your faith in Christ?

_____

_____

_____

12. Paul mentions a kind of boldness that believers should have in being radiant before others. What does this mean? How are you living out this kind of boldness?

_____

_____

_____

LIFE LESSONS

It's been said the Christian life isn't merely difficult—it's *impossible*! Impossible, that is, without supernatural help. Imagine being asked to write a three-act Shakespearean play as brilliant as anything the writer ever penned. A ridiculous and unattainable assignment, right? Yes, unless . . . somehow the very spirit of Shakespeare could indwell you and write through you. Then the task *would* be possible. This is precisely what the new covenant promises: the Spirit of God coming to live within us. He makes us spiritually alive and gives us a new nature and new desires (see 2 Corinthians 5:17). And with all that, he supplies new power to live as God commands.

DEVOTION

God, we praise you for the wonderful promise of the new covenant! What we were unable to do, you did. Show us more and more what grace really means. Grant us insight and humility so we might shine for you, reflect your glory to others, and bring you more glory in the process.

JOURNALING

What does real, God-honoring freedom look like in my life?

_____

_____

_____

_____

_____

_____

_____

_____

FOR FURTHER READING

To complete the book of 2 Corinthians during this twelve-part study, read 2 Corinthians 2:14–3:18. For more Bible passages on the new covenant, read Exodus 34:28–35; Jeremiah 31:31–34; Ezekiel 36:24–29; Romans 7:1–6; and Hebrews 8:1–13.

LESSON FOUR

SHINING THE LIGHT

*God, who said, "Let light shine out of darkness," made
his light shine in our hearts to give us the light of the
knowledge of God's glory displayed in the face of Christ.*
2 CORINTHIANS 4:6

REFLECTION

We all have motives—those reasons (whether conscious or subconscious) for why we do what we do. What would you say are your dominant motivations in life . . . those compelling urges that prompt you to do certain things during the average day?

SITUATION

In this next section, Paul continues to defend his ministry by addressing some other charges made against him—that he had used deceitful means in ministering to the church and that he had preached a gospel only for a "spiritually minded elite" group of people. These charges Paul flatly denies, stating he has set forth the message of Christ plainly—though he acknowledges Satan has blinded many to this truth. Paul concludes by taking about his true motives: to shine the light of Christ into a dark world and proclaim God's glory.

OBSERVATION

*Read 2 Corinthians 4:1–15 from the New International
Version or the New King James Version.*

NEW INTERNATIONAL VERSION
[1] Therefore, since through God's mercy we have this ministry, we do not lose heart. [2] Rather, we have renounced secret and shameful ways; we do not use deception, nor do we distort the word of God. On the

contrary, by setting forth the truth plainly we commend ourselves to everyone's conscience in the sight of God. [3] And even if our gospel is veiled, it is veiled to those who are perishing. [4] The god of this age has blinded the minds of unbelievers, so that they cannot see the light of the gospel that displays the glory of Christ, who is the image of God. [5] For what we preach is not ourselves, but Jesus Christ as Lord, and ourselves as your servants for Jesus' sake. [6] For God, who said, "Let light shine out of darkness," made his light shine in our hearts to give us the light of the knowledge of God's glory displayed in the face of Christ.

[7] But we have this treasure in jars of clay to show that this all-surpassing power is from God and not from us. [8] We are hard pressed on every side, but not crushed; perplexed, but not in despair; [9] persecuted, but not abandoned; struck down, but not destroyed. [10] We always carry around in our body the death of Jesus, so that the life of Jesus may also be revealed in our body. [11] For we who are alive are always being given over to death for Jesus' sake, so that his life may also be revealed in our mortal body. [12] So then, death is at work in us, but life is at work in you.

[13] It is written: "I believed; therefore I have spoken." Since we have that same spirit of faith, we also believe and therefore speak, [14] because we know that the one who raised the Lord Jesus from the dead will also raise us with Jesus and present us with you to himself. [15] All this is for your benefit, so that the grace that is reaching more and more people may cause thanksgiving to overflow to the glory of God.

NEW KING JAMES VERSION

[1] Therefore, since we have this ministry, as we have received mercy, we do not lose heart. [2] But we have renounced the hidden things of shame, not walking in craftiness nor handling the word of God deceitfully, but by manifestation of the truth commending ourselves to every man's conscience in the sight of God. [3] But even if our gospel is veiled, it is veiled to those who are perishing, [4] whose minds the god of this age has blinded, who do not believe, lest the light of the gospel of the glory of Christ, who is the image of God, should shine on them. [5] For we do

not preach ourselves, but Christ Jesus the Lord, and ourselves your bondservants for Jesus' sake. [6] For it is the God who commanded light to shine out of darkness, who has shone in our hearts to give the light of the knowledge of the glory of God in the face of Jesus Christ.

[7] But we have this treasure in earthen vessels, that the excellence of the power may be of God and not of us. [8] We are hard-pressed on every side, yet not crushed; we are perplexed, but not in despair; [9] persecuted, but not forsaken; struck down, but not destroyed— [10] always carrying about in the body the dying of the Lord Jesus, that the life of Jesus also may be manifested in our body. [11] For we who live are always delivered to death for Jesus' sake, that the life of Jesus also may be manifested in our mortal flesh. [12] So then death is working in us, but life in you.

[13] And since we have the same spirit of faith, according to what is written, "I believed and therefore I spoke," we also believe and therefore speak, [14] knowing that He who raised up the Lord Jesus will also raise us up with Jesus, and will present us with you. [15] For all things are for your sakes, that grace, having spread through the many, may cause thanksgiving to abound to the glory of God.

EXPLORATION

1. In a world obsessed with image, it can be difficult to remain authentic. Why is absolute honesty essential for those who serve God?

_____

_____

_____

2. What are some of the ways the devil blinds people to God's truth?

_____

_____

_____

3. Why does Paul compare himself (and all Christians) to "jars of clay" (NIV) or "earthen vessels" (NKJV)?

_____

_____

_____

4. Paul lived a life filled with trouble and hardships of all kinds. Why do you think God allowed such difficulties for one of his most faithful servants?

_____

_____

_____

5. What enabled Paul to speak and proclaim the gospel in spite of these sufferings?

_____

_____

_____

6. How could Paul say everything he had endured was for the Corinthian believers' benefit?

_____

_____

_____

INSPIRATION

Moses asked to see it on Sinai.

It billowed through the temple, leaving priests too stunned to minister.

When Ezekiel saw it, he had to bow.

It encircled the angels and star-struck the shepherds in the Bethlehem pasture.

Jesus radiates it.

John beheld it.

Peter witnessed it on Transfiguration Hill.

Christ will return enthroned in it.

Heaven will be illuminated by it.

It gulf-streams the Atlantic of Scripture, touching every person with the potential of changing every life. Including yours. One glimpse, one taste, one sampling, and your faith will never be the same . . .

Glory. God's glory.

To seek God's glory is to pray, "Thicken the air with your presence; make it misty with your majesty. Part heaven's drape and let your nature spill forth. God, show us God. Part heaven's drapes, and let your nature spill forth. God, show us God."

What the word *Alps* does for the mountains of Europe, *glory* does for God's nature. *Alps* encompasses a host of beauties: creeks, peaks, falling leaves, running elk. To ask to see the Alps is to ask to see it all. To ask to see God's glory is to ask to see all of God. God's glory carries the full weight of his attributes: his love, his character, his strength, and on and on. . . .

The Hebrew term for glory descends from a root word meaning heavy, weighty, or important. God's glory, then, celebrates his significance, his uniqueness, his one-of-a-kindness. As Moses prayed, "Who among the gods is like you, O LORD? Who is like you—majestic in holiness, awesome in glory, working wonders?" (Exodus 15:11).

When you think "God's glory," think "preeminence." And when you think "preeminence," think "priority." For God's glory is God's priority.

God's staff meetings, if he had them, would revolve around one question: "How can we reveal my glory today?" God's to-do list consists of one item: "Reveal my glory." Heaven's framed and mounted purpose statement hangs in the angels' break room just above the angel food cake. It reads: "Declare God's glory."

God exists to *showcase God.* (From *It's Not About Me* by Max Lucado.)

REACTION

7. God created people to live for his glory (see Isaiah 43:7), but in reality, this is not most people's primary concern. What *are* they living for instead?

_____

_____

_____

_____

8. What is the "treasure" you have from God (verse 7)? What are you supposed to do with it?

_____

_____

_____

_____

9. How does knowing you possess this ultimate treasure allow you to view your trials and struggles in a different light—as Paul was able to do?

_____

_____

_____

_____

_____

10. In this passage, Paul makes a big deal about speaking for and about God. How much do you do this in your life? How could you do this more?

_____

_____

_____

_____

11. The Latin phrase *soli deo gloria* means "to the glory of God alone." What are some indications a believer has embraced such a mindset and lifestyle?

_____

_____

_____

12. What are some things you can do right now to shine Christ's glory into the world?

_____

_____

_____

LIFE LESSONS

You can get attention by being slick and flashy and by cultivating a certain image, but you'll never have a deep impact on others that way. The most powerful and eternally significant individuals are those who, like Paul, realize they are mere vessels who have been filled with a heaven-sent treasure. They realize *God* is the point, not them. According to the Bible, we exist to bring God glory, shine for him, and point others to him. Like John the Baptist, we need to say, "He must become greater; I must become less" (John 3:30). We need focus today on the substance of our lives more so than on mere style. Spiritual depth, authenticity, faithfulness—these are the qualities that honor God and cause others to stop and stare.

DEVOTION

Father, forgive us for our tendency to think more highly of ourselves than we should. Forgive us for the times we pursue our agenda and fail to put you first. Remind us that we are clay pots containing the treasure of the gospel. Give us an eternal perspective and mindset so that we are more motivated to live for your glory instead of our own.

JOURNALING

What strength and encouragement do you need from God today to stay focused on the task that he has set for you?

FOR FURTHER READING

To complete the book of 2 Corinthians during this twelve-part study, read 2 Corinthians 4:1–15. For more Bible passages on living for God's glory, read Exodus 33:12–23; 1 Chronicles 16:23–27; 2 Chronicles 7:1–3; Psalm 57:1–11; Psalm 115:1–18; and 1 Corinthians 10:31–33.

LESSON FIVE

ETERNAL PERSPECTIVE

*We do not look at the things which are seen,
but at the things which are not seen. For the
things which are seen are temporary, but the
things which are not seen are eternal.*
2 Corinthians 4:18 NKJV

REFLECTION

More people than ever are living long enough to celebrate their one hundredth birthday. But even a century in this world is still just a blip when you compare it to an eternity in the next. When in your life have you had the most acute sense of "this life is not all there is"?

_____

_____

_____

_____

_____

_____

SITUATION

Paul has now defended his motives in ministering among the Corinthian believers and explained how the weight of message he is carrying has motivated him to persevere in sharing the gospel in the midst of the most overwhelming circumstances. In this next section of his letter, he elaborates on the eternal hope that he has found in Christ—a hope that has changed his perspective on the things of this world and enables him to focus on what truly matters.

OBSERVATION

Read 2 Corinthians 4:16–5:10 from the New International Version or the New King James Version.

NEW INTERNATIONAL VERSION

4:16 Therefore we do not lose heart. Though outwardly we are wasting away, yet inwardly we are being renewed day by day. 17 For our light and momentary troubles are achieving for us an eternal glory that far outweighs them all. [18] So we fix our eyes not on what is seen, but on what is unseen, since what is seen is temporary, but what is unseen is eternal.

[5:1] For we know that if the earthly tent we live in is destroyed, we have a building from God, an eternal house in heaven, not built by human hands. [2] Meanwhile we groan, longing to be clothed instead with our heavenly dwelling, [3] because when we are clothed, we will not be found naked. [4] For while we are in this tent, we groan and are burdened, because we do not wish to be unclothed but to be clothed instead with our heavenly dwelling, so that what is mortal may be swallowed up by life. [5] Now the one who has fashioned us for this very purpose is God, who has given us the Spirit as a deposit, guaranteeing what is to come.

[6] Therefore we are always confident and know that as long as we are at home in the body we are away from the Lord. [7] For we live by faith, not by sight. [8] We are confident, I say, and would prefer to be away from the body and at home with the Lord. [9] So we make it our goal to please him, whether we are at home in the body or away from it. [10] For we must all appear before the judgment seat of Christ, so that each of us may receive what is due us for the things done while in the body, whether good or bad.

NEW KING JAMES VERSION

[4:16] Therefore we do not lose heart. Even though our outward man is perishing, yet the inward man is being renewed day by day. [17] For our light affliction, which is but for a moment, is working for us a far more exceeding and eternal weight of glory, [18] while we do not look at the things which are seen, but at the things which are not seen. For the things which are seen are temporary, but the things which are not seen are eternal.

[5:1] For we know that if our earthly house, this tent, is destroyed, we have a building from God, a house not made with hands, eternal in the heavens. [2] For in this we groan, earnestly desiring to be clothed with our habitation which is from heaven, [3] if indeed, having been clothed, we shall not be found naked. [4] For we who are in this tent groan, being burdened, not because we want to be unclothed, but further clothed, that mortality may be swallowed up by life. [5] Now He who has prepared us for this very thing is God, who also has given us the Spirit as a guarantee.

[6] So we are always confident, knowing that while we are at home in the body we are absent from the Lord. [7] For we walk by faith, not by sight. [8] We are confident, yes, well pleased rather to be absent from the body and to be present with the Lord.

[9] Therefore we make it our aim, whether present or absent, to be well pleasing to Him. [10] For we must all appear before the judgment seat of Christ, that each one may receive the things done in the body, according to what he has done, whether good or bad.

EXPLORATION

1. What was Paul's secret in getting through the hard times of life and ministry?

_____

_____

_____

2. What does it mean in verse 18 to "fix our eyes" (NIV) or "look at the things which are not seen" (NKJV)? How can you personally apply this to your life?

_____

_____

_____

3. What does Paul mean by comparing an earthly body to a tent? What is he saying about the state of a believer's life on this earth?

_____

_____

_____

4. How can you balance longing for heaven with the need to accomplish God's purposes for you here on earth?

_____

_____

_____

5. What are some ways that seek to maintain an eternal perspective? How are you walking by faith and not by sight?

_____

_____

_____

6. In Jeremiah 31:34, God states that he forgets your sins once you are forgiven under the terms of the new covenant. Given this, why does Paul mention the judgment seat of Christ?

_____

_____

_____

INSPIRATION

Groan. The dreaded standby list. The equivalent of baseball tryouts—on the field but not on the team. Possibility but no guarantee. Standby passengers punctuate every thought with a question mark. _Am I condemned to a life of airport food? Will the Sky Club accept my credit card? Is this why they call an airport a terminal?_

Ticketed passengers, by contrast, relax like a teacher on the first day of summer. They read magazines and thumb through newspapers. Every so often they lift their eyes to pity us, the standby peasantry. Oh, to be numbered among the confirmed. To have my very own seat number and departure time. How can you rest if you aren't assured passage on the final flight home?

Many people don't. Many Christians don't. They live with a deep-seated anxiety about eternity. They *think* they are saved, *hope* they are saved, but still they doubt, wondering, *Am I* really *saved*?

This is not merely an academic question. Children who accept Christ ask it. Parents of prodigals ask it. So do friends of the wayward. It surfaces in the heart of the struggler. It seeps into the thoughts of the dying. When we forget our vow to God, does God forget us? Does God place us on a standby list?

Our behavior gives us reason to wonder. We are strong one day, weak the next. Devoted one hour, flagging the next. Believing, then unbelieving. Our lives mirror the contours of a roller coaster, highs and lows.

Conventional wisdom draws a line through the middle of these fluctuations. Perform above this line, and enjoy God's acceptance. But dip below it, and expect a pink slip from heaven. In this paradigm a person is lost and saved multiple times a day, in and out of the kingdom on a regular basis. Salvation becomes a matter of timing. You just hope you die on an upswing. No security, stability, or confidence.

This is not God's plan. He draws the line, for sure. But he draws it beneath our ups and downs. Jesus' language couldn't be stronger: "I give them eternal life, and they shall never perish; no one will snatch them out of my hand" (John 10:28).

Jesus promised a new life that could not be forfeited or terminated. "Whoever hears my word and believes him who sent me has eternal life and will not be judged but has crossed over from death to life" (John 5:24). Bridges are burned, and the transfer is accomplished. Ebbs and flows continue, but they never disqualify. Ups and downs may mark our days, but they will never ban us from his kingdom. Jesus bottom-lines our lives with grace.

Even more, God stakes his claim on us. "By his Spirit he has stamped us with his eternal pledge—a sure beginning of what he is destined to complete" (2 Corinthians 1:22 MSG). You've done something similar: engraved your name on a valued ring, etched your identity on a tool or iPad. Cowboys brand cattle with the mark of the ranch. Stamping declares ownership. Through his Spirit, God stamps us. Would-be takers are repelled by the presence of his name. Satan is driven back by the declaration: *Hands off. This child is mine! Eternally, God.* (From *Grace* by Max Lucado.)

REACTION

7. Why do some believers in Christ live with a deep-seated anxiety about eternity? What are your feelings about the end of life and the next world to come?

_____

_____

_____

8. How has knowing that you are a "ticketed passenger" to eternal life helped you fix your gaze on God and the blessings he has provided?

_____

_____

_____

9. The judgment seat of Christ will be a place of eternal reward for faithful believers. What kinds of reward should you expect (see 1 Corinthians 9:25–27, James 1:12, and 1 Peter 1:3–5)?

_____

_____

_____

10. How does it affect the way you act today to know that one day you will stand before Christ and be held accountable for what you have done on this earth?

_____

_____

_____

11. What promise do you have if God's Spirit is present within you?

_____

_____

_____

12. What are some specific changes you need to make in your life so you can honestly say, "My only goal is to please God"?

_____

_____

_____

LIFE LESSONS

A clear and compelling vision of the future has real power to affect our actions in the present. Think of the student who stands to get a scholarship if he or she can achieve a certain SAT score next month, or the bride-to-be who wants to fit into her wedding gown in six weeks, or the hardworking couple who is absolutely committed to the goal of retiring by age fifty. The apostle Paul was riveted by the reality of eternity: the judgment seat of Christ helped him shape his behavior, and the promise of heaven gave him real hope when life's circumstances turned unpleasant. By cultivating a mindset that continually recalls these easy-to-forget realities, we become the people God made us to be and our lives take on new power and purpose.

DEVOTION

Lord, we confess how quickly we lose sight of ultimate realities and how easily we become immersed in temporal events. Thank you for Paul's valuable reminder that this life is not all there is. Thank you for the promise of heaven. Show us how to set our minds on things above, not on the things that are on the earth.

JOURNALING

C.S. Lewis suggested the people who do the most in this world are those who think the most of the next world. When have you been most motivated and energized by an eternal perspective?

FOR FURTHER READING

To complete the book of 2 Corinthians during this twelve-part study, read 2 Corinthians 4:16–5:21. For more Bible passages on eternal perspective, read Job 19:25–27; Psalm 73:24– 26; John 15:1–4; 1 Thessalonians 4:13–18; and Revelation 21–22.

LESSON SIX

LIVING AS A SERVANT

We put no stumbling block in anyone's path, so that
our ministry will not be discredited. Rather, as servants
of God we commend ourselves in every way.

2 Corinthians 6:3–4

REFLECTION

Perhaps you've heard the old saying, "If you were arrested and put on trial for being a devoted follower of Christ, would there be enough evidence to convict you?" What are the biggest changes you've seen God make in your life since you put your faith in Jesus?

_____

_____

_____

_____

_____

_____

SITUATION

For Paul, the time of God's favor was _now_—in the present—for he had sent his Son into the world to die for humanity's sins and receive salvation. It was this understanding that compelled him to urge the Corinthian believers to not receive God's grace in vain. Paul wanted them to accept this gift of God's grace and, by their actions, show that they were new creations in Christ. This involved not only putting aside the former sinful lives, but reflecting God's glory to the world through acts of genuine love regardless of what life threw at them.

OBSERVATION

Read 2 Corinthians 6:1–10 from the New International Version or the New King James Version.

NEW INTERNATIONAL VERSION

[1] As God's co-workers we urge you not to receive God's grace in vain.
[2] For he says,

"In the time of my favor I heard you,
    and in the day of salvation I helped you."

I tell you, now is the time of God's favor, now is the day of salvation.

[3] We put no stumbling block in anyone's path, so that our ministry will not be discredited. [4] Rather, as servants of God we commend ourselves in every way: in great endurance; in troubles, hardships and distresses; [5] in beatings, imprisonments and riots; in hard work, sleepless nights and hunger; [6] in purity, understanding, patience and kindness; in the Holy Spirit and in sincere love; [7] in truthful speech and in the power of God; with weapons of righteousness in the right hand and in the left; [8] through glory and dishonor, bad report and good report; genuine, yet regarded as impostors; [9] known, yet regarded as unknown; dying, and yet we live on; beaten, and yet not killed; [10] sorrowful, yet always rejoicing; poor, yet making many rich; having nothing, and yet possessing everything.

New King James Version

[1] We then, as workers together with Him also plead with you not to receive the grace of God in vain. [2] For He says:

"In an acceptable time I have heard you,
    And in the day of salvation I have helped you."

Behold, now is the accepted time; behold, now is the day of salvation.

[3] We give no offense in anything, that our ministry may not be blamed. [4] But in all things we commend ourselves as ministers of God: in much patience, in tribulations, in needs, in distresses, [5] in stripes, in imprisonments, in tumults, in labors, in sleeplessness, in fastings; [6] by purity, by knowledge, by longsuffering, by kindness, by the Holy Spirit, by sincere love, [7] by the word of truth, by the power of God, by the armor of righteousness on the right hand and on the left, [8] by honor and dishonor, by evil report and good report; as deceivers, and yet true;

⁹ as unknown, and yet well known; as dying, and behold we live; as chastened, and yet not killed; ¹⁰ as sorrowful, yet always rejoicing; as poor, yet making many rich; as having nothing, and yet possessing all things.

EXPLORATION

1. Paul describes himself (and his colleagues) as "God's co-workers" (verse 1) and "servants of God" (verse 4). What is the difference?

_____

_____

_____

2. What does it mean to receive God's grace in vain?

_____

_____

_____

3. How does Paul's willingness to endure suffering for the sake of Christ prove that he "put no stumbling block in anyone's path" (verse 3)?

_____

_____

_____

4. What are some of the ways that Paul and his fellow ministers of the gospel "commended" themselves to the people they served?

_____

_____

_____

_____

5. Paul notes that a role of a servant of God is to persevere and endure even in the midst of struggles. But what internal qualities does a servant also need to possess (see verses 6–7)?

_____

_____

_____

6. How does living a blameless life before God give a believer freedom?

_____

_____

_____

INSPIRATION

God's cure for the common life includes a strong dose of servanthood. Timely reminder. As you celebrate your unique design, be careful. Don't be so focused on what you love to do that you neglect what needs to be done.

A 3:00 AM diaper change fits in very few sweet spots. Most stories don't feature the strength of garage sweeping. Visiting your sick neighbor might not come naturally to you. Still, the sick need to be encouraged, garages need sweeping, and diapers need changing.

The world needs servants. People like Jesus, who "did not come to be served, but to serve" (Matthew 20:28). He chose remote Nazareth over center-stage Jerusalem, his dad's carpentry shop over a marble-columned palace, and three decades of anonymity over a life of popularity.

Jesus came to serve. He selected prayer over sleep, the wilderness over the Jordan, irascible apostles over obedient angels. I'd have gone with the angels. Given the choice, I would have built my apostle team out of cherubim and seraphim or Gabriel and Michael, eyewitnesses of Red Sea rescues and Mount Carmel falling fires. I'd choose the angels.

Not Jesus. He picked the people. Peter, Andrew, John, and Matthew. When they feared the storm, he stilled it. When they had no coin for taxes, he supplied it. And when they had no wine for the wedding or food for the multitude, he made both. He came to serve. . . .

He let a woman in Samaria interrupt his rest, a woman in adultery interrupt his sermon, a woman with a disease interrupt his plans, and one with remorse interrupt his meal.

Though none of the apostles washed his feet, he washed theirs. Though none of the soldiers at the cross begged for mercy, he extended it. And though his followers skedaddled like scared rabbits on Thursday, he came searching for them on Easter Sunday. The resurrected King ascended to heaven only after he'd spent forty days with his friends— teaching them, encouraging them . . . serving them.

Why? It's what he came to do. He came to serve. . . .

Every day do something you don't want to do. Pick up someone else's trash. Surrender your parking place. Call the long-winded relative. Carry the cooler. Doesn't have to be a big thing. Helen Keller once told the Tennessee legislature that when she was young, she had longed to do great things and could not, so she decided to do small things in a great way. Don't be too big to do something small. "Throw yourselves into the work of the Master, confident that nothing you do for him is a waste of time or effort" (1 Corinthians 15:58 MSG). (From *Cure for the Common Life* by Max Lucado.)

REACTION

7. Why do you think many Christians are reluctant to roll up their sleeves and minister to others?

_____

_____

_____

_____

_____

LIVING AS A SERVANT

8. What ironies and paradoxes does Paul cite as he describes his complicated, roller-coaster life as a committed servant of Christ?

_____

_____

_____

_____

_____

_____

_____

9. Some people protest that Paul's words only apply to "full-time ministers," and that the average Christian can't be expected to live like this. How do you respond to this claim?

_____

_____

_____

_____

_____

_____

_____

10. Paul was devoted to living in such a way that his life did not contradict the gospel. What attitudes, values, actions, or habits can tarnish the reputation of Christ or his church?

_____

_____

_____

_____

_____

_____

11. What link did Paul see between undergoing affliction and developing into a productive servant of God? What did Paul learn through his trials?

_____

_____

_____

12. Why, in the final analysis, does being a servant matter so much?

_____

_____

_____

LIFE LESSONS

The more Adam and Eve pondered the lies of the evil one, the more they doubted the goodness of God. Finally, declaring their independence, they struck out on their own to try to find "life"—to make it work without God. They would do this by trying to control situations and people. Aren't we chips off the old block? Don't we approach life the same way? Enter Jesus, who says, "Whoever wants to save their life will lose it, but whoever loses their life for me will find it" (Matthew 16:25). In other words, the path to joy and fulfillment isn't found in _control_ but in _surrender_. Those who choose to be servants of God, giving up control and yielding fully to his will and his work, are those who find true life—now and forever.

DEVOTION

Father, we can either live selfishly, saying, "Our will be done," or we can live as servants, saying, "Your will be done." Please change us. Make us more like Paul, and more like your own Son, Christ. Remind us that we are not our own, but that we have been bought at a price.

JOURNALING

How can you use the gifts that you have been given to better serve as a
faithful steward of God's grace (see 1 Peter 4:10–11)?

_____

_____

_____

_____

_____

_____

_____

_____

_____

_____

_____

_____

_____

_____

_____

_____

_____

_____

_____

_____

_____

_____

_____

_____

_____

_____

_____

_____

FOR FURTHER READING

To complete the book of 2 Corinthians during this twelve-part study, read 2 Corinthians 6:1–7:1. For more Bible passages on servanthood, read Matthew 10:24–25; 20:26; Luke 19:11–27; John 15:18–25; and Philippians 2:5–11.

FOLLOW THE LEADER

For even if I made you sorry with my letter, I do not regret it. . . . Now I rejoice, not that you were made sorry, but that your sorrow led to repentance.

2 Corinthians 7:8–9 NKJV

REFLECTION

Consider for a moment all the books you have seen that have to do with *leadership*. Clearly, this is a hot topic! In your opinion, what are the qualities that make for the best leaders?

_____

_____

_____

_____

_____

_____

SITUATION

As Paul progresses in his letter, it becomes clear that some had accused him of bringing about the moral and financial ruin of individuals in Corinth by exploiting them. To Paul's sorrow, some in the church had, at least in part, fallen prey to these rumors. In refuting these charges, Paul again reminds the believers of the work that he did among them for their benefit—and, in the process, highlights some key traits of effective and godly leaders.

OBSERVATION

Read 2 Corinthians 7:2–16 from the New International Version or the New King James Version.

NEW INTERNATIONAL VERSION

² Make room for us in your hearts. We have wronged no one, we have corrupted no one, we have exploited no one. ³ I do not say this to condemn you; I have said before that you have such a place in our hearts that we would live or die with you. ⁴ I have spoken to you with great

frankness; I take great pride in you. I am greatly encouraged; in all our troubles my joy knows no bounds.

[5] For when we came into Macedonia, we had no rest, but we were harassed at every turn—conflicts on the outside, fears within. [6] But God, who comforts the downcast, comforted us by the coming of Titus, [7] and not only by his coming but also by the comfort you had given him. He told us about your longing for me, your deep sorrow, your ardent concern for me, so that my joy was greater than ever.

[8] Even if I caused you sorrow by my letter, I do not regret it. Though I did regret it—I see that my letter hurt you, but only for a little while— [9] yet now I am happy, not because you were made sorry, but because your sorrow led you to repentance. For you became sorrowful as God intended and so were not harmed in any way by us. [10] Godly sorrow brings repentance that leads to salvation and leaves no regret, but worldly sorrow brings death. [11] See what this godly sorrow has produced in you: what earnestness, what eagerness to clear yourselves, what indignation, what alarm, what longing, what concern, what readiness to see justice done. At every point you have proved yourselves to be innocent in this matter. [12] So even though I wrote to you, it was neither on account of the one who did the wrong nor on account of the injured party, but rather that before God you could see for yourselves how devoted to us you are. [13] By all this we are encouraged.

In addition to our own encouragement, we were especially delighted to see how happy Titus was, because his spirit has been refreshed by all of you. [14] I had boasted to him about you, and you have not embarrassed me. But just as everything we said to you was true, so our boasting about you to Titus has proved to be true as well. [15] And his affection for you is all the greater when he remembers that you were all obedient, receiving him with fear and trembling. [16] I am glad I can have complete confidence in you.

New King James Version
[2] Open your hearts to us. We have wronged no one, we have corrupted no one, we have cheated no one. [3] I do not say this to condemn; for I

have said before that you are in our hearts, to die together and to live together. ⁴ Great is my boldness of speech toward you, great is my boasting on your behalf. I am filled with comfort. I am exceedingly joyful in all our tribulation.

⁵ For indeed, when we came to Macedonia, our bodies had no rest, but we were troubled on every side. Outside were conflicts, inside were fears. ⁶ Nevertheless God, who comforts the downcast, comforted us by the coming of Titus, ⁷ and not only by his coming, but also by the consolation with which he was comforted in you, when he told us of your earnest desire, your mourning, your zeal for me, so that I rejoiced even more.

⁸ For even if I made you sorry with my letter, I do not regret it; though I did regret it. For I perceive that the same epistle made you sorry, though only for a while. ⁹ Now I rejoice, not that you were made sorry, but that your sorrow led to repentance. For you were made sorry in a godly manner, that you might suffer loss from us in nothing. ¹⁰ For godly sorrow produces repentance leading to salvation, not to be regretted; but the sorrow of the world produces death. ¹¹ For observe this very thing, that you sorrowed in a godly manner: What diligence it produced in you, what clearing of yourselves, what indignation, what fear, what vehement desire, what zeal, what vindication! In all things you proved yourselves to be clear in this matter. ¹² Therefore, although I wrote to you, I did not do it for the sake of him who had done the wrong, nor for the sake of him who suffered wrong, but that our care for you in the sight of God might appear to you.

¹³ Therefore we have been comforted in your comfort. And we rejoiced exceedingly more for the joy of Titus, because his spirit has been refreshed by you all. ¹⁴ For if in anything I have boasted to him about you, I am not ashamed. But as we spoke all things to you in truth, even so our boasting to Titus was found true. ¹⁵ And his affections are greater for you as he remembers the obedience of you all, how with fear and trembling you received him. ¹⁶ Therefore I rejoice that I have confidence in you in everything.

EXPLORATION

1. Paul mentions being proud of the Corinthians (see verse 4). When is the last time a leader or authority figure expressed this to you? How did those words affect you?

_____

_____

_____

2. How does Paul's defense of his ministry in this passage correspond to Jesus' classic statement, "You will know these people by what they do" (Matthew 7:16 NCV)?

_____

_____

_____

3. What are some ways a leader can lose the trust of his or her followers?

_____

_____

_____

4. Why did Paul say that he did not regret writing a severe letter of correction to the believers in Corinth? What did he see as the end result of that letter?

_____

_____

_____

5. What valuable lessons about confrontation do you find in this passage?

_____

_____

_____

6. How did Paul end this section of his letter? Why did he feel it was important to express his confidence in the Corinthian believers?

_____

_____

_____

INSPIRATION

Peer into the prison and see him for yourself: bent and frail, shackled to the arm of a Roman guard. Behold the apostle of God. Who knows when his back last felt a bed or his mouth knew a good meal? Three decades of travel and trouble, and what's he got to show for it?

There's squabbling in Philippi, competition in Corinth, the legalists are swarming in Galatia. Crete is plagued by money-grabbers. Ephesus is stalked by womanizers. Even some of Paul's own friends have turned against him.

Dead broke. No family. No property. Nearsighted and worn out.

Oh, he had his moments. Spoke to an emperor once, but couldn't convert him. Gave a lecture at an Areopagus men's club, but wasn't asked to speak there again. Spent a few days with Peter and the boys in Jerusalem, but they couldn't seem to get along, so Paul hit the road.

And never got off. Ephesus, Thessalonica, Athens, Syracuse, Malta. The only list longer than his itinerary was his misfortune. Got stoned in one city and stranded in another. Nearly drowned as many times as he nearly starved. If he spent more than one week in the same place, it was probably a prison.

He never received a salary. Had to pay his own travel expenses. Kept a part-time job on the side to make ends meet.

Doesn't look like a hero.

Doesn't sound like one either. He introduced himself as the worst sinner in history. He was a Christian-killer before he was a Christian leader. At times his heart was so heavy, Paul's pen drug itself across the page. *"What a wretched man I am! Who will rescue me from this body that is subject to death?"* (Romans 7:24).

Only heaven knows how long he stared at the question before he found the courage to defy logic and write, *"Thanks be to God, who delivers me through Jesus Christ our Lord!"* (Romans 7:25).

One minute he's in charge; the next he's in doubt. One day he's preaching; the next he's in prison. And that's where I'd like you to look at him. Look at him in the prison.

Pretend you don't know him. You're a guard or a cook or a friend of the hatchet man, and you've come to get one last look at the guy while they sharpen the blade.

What you see shuffling around in his cell isn't too much. But what I lean over and tell you is: "That man will shape the course of history." (From *When God Whispers Your Name* by Max Lucado.)

REACTION

7. What are some things that made Paul an unlikely leader? What qualities or experiences equipped him for such amazing service as an apostle?

_____

_____

_____

_____

_____

8. What did Paul recognize about his own weaknesses? How do you think his realization of those weaknesses helped him to relate to other believers?

_____

_____

_____

_____

_____

9. The Corinthians were Paul's "problem" church, and he confronted them on many occasions. What gives someone the authority and confidence to confront another person?

_____

_____

_____

10. When is the last time a leader confronted you? How did you respond?

_____

_____

_____

11. How can you be a better follower to those who lead you?

_____

_____

_____

12. Paul concluded this section of his letter by referring to his coworker Titus. What was Titus' role in the church? Why is it so important to share the burden of leadership with others?

_____

_____

_____

LIFE LESSONS

If a leader is one who influences others to go in a specific direction and to achieve certain goals, then everyone can and should be a leader. A dad can impact his family. A third grader can lead his classmates. A stay-at-home mom can make a difference in the lives of her neighbors. A manager can affect those in the office. Paul's example reminds us that effective, God-honoring leadership is rooted in honesty, integrity, genuine concern, courage, and straightforward communication. Everyone has the capacity to lead someone else, and everyone has the need also to follow another. Remember, the one who is unwilling to follow is unfit to lead.

DEVOTION

Father, thank you for the strong leaders you've put in our lives. None of them are perfect, but all have strengths from which we can benefit. Remind us often to pray for them—and give us opportunities to encourage them in tangible and concrete ways.

JOURNALING

What are some ways that you have found to be an effective leader to others?

_____

_____

_____

_____

_____

_____

_____

_____

_____

_____

_____

_____

_____

_____

_____

FOR FURTHER READING

To complete the book of 2 Corinthians during this twelve-part study, read 2 Corinthians 7:2–16. For more Bible passages on biblical leadership, read Exodus 18:13–25; Titus 1:1–16; 1 Timothy 3:1–13; James 3:1–2; and Hebrews 13:17–19.

MONEY MATTERS

*Each of you should give what you have decided
in your heart to give, not reluctantly or under
compulsion, for God loves a cheerful giver.*

2 CORINTHIANS 9:7

71

REFLECTION

Passing the plate . . . asking for money . . . sermons on tithing . . . few topics generate more raised eyebrows, more tension, or more shakes of the head than this one. Why do you think giving is such a sore subject for so many Christians?

_____

_____

_____

_____

_____

_____

SITUATION

In this section of Paul's letter, he pauses from defending his character and ministry to remind the believers of a matter that is close to his heart: the collection for poverty-stricken church in Jerusalem. This was not the first time that Paul had written to the Corinthians about this project (see 1 Corinthians 16:1–4), but it appears that progress on the collection had ground to a halt, and he needed to remind them again of its importance. The resulting instructions from Paul comprise the lengthiest and most detailed teaching on giving in the New Testament.

OBSERVATION

Read 2 Corinthians 9:1–15 from the New International Version or the New King James Version.

NEW INTERNATIONAL VERSION
[1] There is no need for me to write to you about this service to the Lord's people. [2] For I know your eagerness to help, and I have been boasting

about it to the Macedonians, telling them that since last year you in Achaia were ready to give; and your enthusiasm has stirred most of them to action. ³ But I am sending the brothers in order that our boasting about you in this matter should not prove hollow, but that you may be ready, as I said you would be. ⁴ For if any Macedonians come with me and find you unprepared, we—not to say anything about you—would be ashamed of having been so confident. ⁵ So I thought it necessary to urge the brothers to visit you in advance and finish the arrangements for the generous gift you had promised. Then it will be ready as a generous gift, not as one grudgingly given.

⁶ Remember this: Whoever sows sparingly will also reap sparingly, and whoever sows generously will also reap generously. ⁷ Each of you should give what you have decided in your heart to give, not reluctantly or under compulsion, for God loves a cheerful giver. ⁸ And God is able to bless you abundantly, so that in all things at all times, having all that you need, you will abound in every good work. ⁹ As it is written:

"They have freely scattered their gifts to the poor;
their righteousness endures forever."

¹⁰ Now he who supplies seed to the sower and bread for food will also supply and increase your store of seed and will enlarge the harvest of your righteousness. ¹¹ You will be enriched in every way so that you can be generous on every occasion, and through us your generosity will result in thanksgiving to God.

¹² This service that you perform is not only supplying the needs of the Lord's people but is also overflowing in many expressions of thanks to God. ¹³ Because of the service by which you have proved yourselves, others will praise God for the obedience that accompanies your confession of the gospel of Christ, and for your generosity in sharing with them and with everyone else. ¹⁴ And in their prayers for you their hearts will go out to you, because of the surpassing grace God has given you. ¹⁵ Thanks be to God for his indescribable gift!

New King James Version

¹ Now concerning the ministering to the saints, it is superfluous for me to write to you; ² for I know your willingness, about which I boast of you to the Macedonians, that Achaia was ready a year ago; and your zeal has stirred up the majority. ³ Yet I have sent the brethren, lest our boasting of you should be in vain in this respect, that, as I said, you may be ready; ⁴ lest if some Macedonians come with me and find you unprepared, we (not to mention you!) should be ashamed of this confident boasting. ⁵ Therefore I thought it necessary to exhort the brethren to go to you ahead of time, and prepare your generous gift beforehand, which you had previously promised, that it may be ready as a matter of generosity and not as a grudging obligation.

⁶ But this I say: He who sows sparingly will also reap sparingly, and he who sows bountifully will also reap bountifully. ⁷ So let each one give as he purposes in his heart, not grudgingly or of necessity; for God loves a cheerful giver. ⁸ And God is able to make all grace abound toward you, that you, always having all sufficiency in all things, may have an abundance for every good work. ⁹ As it is written:

> "He has dispersed abroad,
> He has given to the poor;
> His righteousness endures forever."

¹⁰ Now may He who supplies seed to the sower, and bread for food, supply and multiply the seed you have sown and increase the fruits of your righteousness, ¹¹ while you are enriched in everything for all liberality, which causes thanksgiving through us to God. ¹² For the administration of this service not only supplies the needs of the saints, but also is abounding through many thanksgivings to God, ¹³ while, through the proof of this ministry, they glorify God for the obedience of your confession to the gospel of Christ, and for your liberal sharing with them and all men, ¹⁴ and by their prayer for you, who long for you because of the exceeding grace of God in you. ¹⁵ Thanks be to God for His indescribable gift!

EXPLORATION

1. How did Paul "boast" about the Corinthians to the other churches? How would this have compelled the Corinthian believers to respond?

_____

_____

_____

2. Does Paul specify an amount or percentage of income that Christians should give? What does he say about this in terms of "sowing" and "reaping"?

_____

_____

_____

3. What does Paul say is more important in giving than just the amount?

_____

_____

_____

4. In what ways does giving demonstrate faith and trust in God?

_____

_____

_____

5. How does this passage support the idea that you can't out-give God?

_____

_____

_____

6. What does Paul say is the result of generous giving? Who does it affect?

_____

_____

_____

INSPIRATION

Think for just a moment about the things you own. Think about the house you have, the car you drive, the money you've saved. Think about the jewelry you've inherited and the stocks you've traded and the clothes you've purchased. Envision all your stuff, and let me remind you of two biblical truths.

Your stuff isn't yours. Ask any coroner. Ask any embalmer. Ask any funeral-home director. No one takes anything with him. When one of the wealthiest men in history, John D. Rockefeller, died, his accountant was asked, "How much did John D. leave?" The accountant's reply? "All of it." ·

"Naked a man comes from his mother's womb, and as he comes, so he departs. He takes nothing from his labor that he can carry in his hand" (Ecclesiastes 5:15).

All that stuff—it's not yours. And you know what else about all that stuff? *It's not you.* Who you are has nothing to do with the clothes you wear or the car you drive. Jesus said, "Life is not defined by what you have, even when you have a lot" (Luke 12:15 MSG). Heaven does not know you as the fellow with the nice suit or the woman with the big house or the kid with the new bike. Heaven knows your heart. "The LORD does not look at the things man looks at. Man looks at the outward appearance, but the LORD looks at the heart" (1 Samuel 16:7).

When God thinks of you, he may see your compassion, your devotion, your tenderness or quick mind, but he doesn't think of your things. And when you think of you, you shouldn't either. Define yourself by your stuff, and you'll feel good when you have a lot and bad when you don't. Contentment comes when we can honestly say with Paul: "I have learned to be content whatever the circumstances. I know what it is to be in need, and I know what it is to have plenty" (Philippians 4:11–12). . . .

You have a God who hears you, the power of love behind you, the Holy Spirit within you, and all of heaven ahead of you. If you have the Shepherd, you have grace for every sin, direction for every turn, a candle for every corner, and an anchor for every storm. You have everything you need. (From *Traveling Light* by Max Lucado.)

REACTION

7. How does a Christian move from *greediness* to *generosity*?

_____

_____

_____

_____

8. How would you describe your current giving habits?

_____

_____

_____

_____

9. How do you determine what churches, ministries, or missionaries to support? How do you determine how much you will give?

_____

_____

_____

_____

10. Why is it possible to give too much or to an unwise degree?

_____

_____

_____

_____

11. Why do some people get unexpected money and automatically think of giving, while others get unanticipated windfalls and immediately think of spending?

_____

_____

_____

_____

12. What advice would you give to a Christian who said, "I know I need to be giving to the Lord's work, but how do I start when I've got so many bills"?

_____

_____

_____

_____

LIFE LESSONS

When it comes to money, most folks tend to think, "Woohoo! What can I buy?" Then, if there's anything left over (which is rare), they save or give a little bit. There's a more biblical model: give first, save second, and spend third. Imagine the long-term implications of such a plan. In the here-and-now, your life would be much less stressful if you embarked on a disciplined plan of saving for upcoming expenses, emergencies, and retirement. By curtailing your spending, you would eliminate the likelihood of piling up consumer debt. And when you arrive in heaven, you would find that hundreds are there because you had the ability to use earthly wealth to help people grasp eternal truth. It's not rocket science. Mishandling money will rob you of joy. Managing it well, so that you can be more generous, will lead to rich blessing.

DEVOTION

God, as we think about money and how to handle it in a way that honors you, give us faith to believe the words of Jesus—that it is more blessed to give than to receive. We want to become more generous and quicker to open up our wallet or checkbook. Help us. Change us.

JOURNALING

When presented with opportunities to give, how do you tend to react?

FOR FURTHER READING

To complete the book of 2 Corinthians during this twelve-part study, read 2 Corinthians 8:1–9:15. For more Bible passages on giving, read Deuteronomy 15:10–11; Malachi 3:8; Matthew 10:8; Luke 6:38; Romans 12:8; Acts 20:35; and 1 Timothy 6:17–19.

LESSON NINE

GROUND ZERO

For the weapons of our warfare are not carnal but mighty in God for pulling down strongholds, casting down arguments and every high thing that exalts itself against the knowledge of God, bringing every thought into captivity to the obedience of Christ.

2 Corinthians 10:4–5 nkjv

REFLECTION

Pick any issue—parenting, money management, relationships, handling conflicts—and you will find a number of different (and often opposing) viewpoints on the subject. Why the wide discrepancy? How can you know the best course of action in such situations?

_____

_____

_____

_____

_____

_____

_____

_____

_____

_____

_____

SITUATION

There can be no doubt that Paul makes an abrupt shift in tone at this point of the letter. Many have wondered the cause for the sudden change, with some even proposing this section actually represents the "severe letter" to which Paul previously referred. However, it is likely Paul simply wrote 2 Corinthians 1–9 over one period time, then distressing news arrived that caused him to again pick up his pen to draft 2 Corinthians 10–13, and then he sent the group together as a single letter. In this section, Paul again defends his ministry and his gospel of grace, reminding the Corinthians that a deeper cosmic battle is taking place—a battle for their hearts and their minds.

OBSERVATION

Read 2 Corinthians 10:1–18 from the New International
Version or the New King James Version.

New International Version

[1] By the humility and gentleness of Christ, I appeal to you—I, Paul, who am "timid" when face to face with you, but "bold" toward you when away! [2] I beg you that when I come I may not have to be as bold as I expect to be toward some people who think that we live by the standards of this world. [3] For though we live in the world, we do not wage war as the world does. [4] The weapons we fight with are not the weapons of the world. On the contrary, they have divine power to demolish strongholds. [5] We demolish arguments and every pretension that sets itself up against the knowledge of God, and we take captive every thought to make it obedient to Christ. [6] And we will be ready to punish every act of disobedience, once your obedience is complete.

[7] You are judging by appearances. If anyone is confident that they belong to Christ, they should consider again that we belong to Christ just as much as they do. [8] So even if I boast somewhat freely about the authority the Lord gave us for building you up rather than tearing you down, I will not be ashamed of it. [9] I do not want to seem to be trying to frighten you with my letters. [10] For some say, "His letters are weighty and forceful, but in person he is unimpressive and his speaking amounts to nothing." [11] Such people should realize that what we are in our letters when we are absent, we will be in our actions when we are present.

[12] We do not dare to classify or compare ourselves with some who commend themselves. When they measure themselves by themselves and compare themselves with themselves, they are not wise. [13] We, however, will not boast beyond proper limits, but will confine our boasting to the sphere of service God himself has assigned to us, a sphere that also includes you. [14] We are not going too far in our boasting, as would be the case if we had not come to you, for we did get as far as you with the gospel

of Christ. [15] Neither do we go beyond our limits by boasting of work done by others. Our hope is that, as your faith continues to grow, our sphere of activity among you will greatly expand, [16] so that we can preach the gospel in the regions beyond you. For we do not want to boast about work already done in someone else's territory. [17] But, "Let the one who boasts boast in the Lord." [18] For it is not the one who commends himself who is approved, but the one whom the Lord commends.

NEW KING JAMES VERSION

[1] Now I, Paul, myself am pleading with you by the meekness and gentleness of Christ—who in presence am lowly among you, but being absent am bold toward you. [2] But I beg you that when I am present I may not be bold with that confidence by which I intend to be bold against some, who think of us as if we walked according to the flesh. [3] For though we walk in the flesh, we do not war according to the flesh. [4] For the weapons of our warfare are not carnal but mighty in God for pulling down strongholds, [5] casting down arguments and every high thing that exalts itself against the knowledge of God, bringing every thought into captivity to the obedience of Christ, [6] and being ready to punish all disobedience when your obedience is fulfilled.

[7] Do you look at things according to the outward appearance? If anyone is convinced in himself that he is Christ's, let him again consider this in himself, that just as he is Christ's, even so we are Christ's. [8] For even if I should boast somewhat more about our authority, which the Lord gave us for edification and not for your destruction, I shall not be ashamed— [9] lest I seem to terrify you by letters. [10] "For his letters," they say, "are weighty and powerful, but his bodily presence is weak, and his speech contemptible." [11] Let such a person consider this, that what we are in word by letters when we are absent, such we will also be in deed when we are present.

[12] For we dare not class ourselves or compare ourselves with those who commend themselves. But they, measuring themselves by themselves, and comparing themselves among themselves, are not wise. [13] We, however, will not boast beyond measure, but within the limits of the

sphere which God appointed us—a sphere which especially includes you. [14] For we are not overextending ourselves (as though our authority did not extend to you), for it was to you that we came with the gospel of Christ; [15] not boasting of things beyond measure, that is, in other men's labors, but having hope, that as your faith is increased, we shall be greatly enlarged by you in our sphere, [16] to preach the gospel in the regions beyond you, and not to boast in another man's sphere of accomplishment.

[17] But "he who glories, let him glory in the Lord." [18] For not he who commends himself is approved, but whom the Lord commends.

EXPLORATION

1. What is the basic argument or conflict taking place in Corinth?

_____

_____

_____

2. Paul asserts that beneath the surface, the enemy (the devil) has a foothold in the church at Corinth. What does this mean? How could such a thing happen?

_____

_____

_____

3. Critics had evidently claimed that Paul was bold in his writings but meek and uncertain when he was with the Corinthians in person. How does Paul refute this charge?

_____

_____

_____

4. How does Paul advocate dealing with wrong thinking and wrong behavior in the church?

_____

_____

_____

5. Paul is not eager to confront those Corinthians who continue to oppose his God-given authority, but he is willing to do what is necessary to preserve the church. Why is this kind of bold leadership important even today?

_____

_____

_____

6. How should you be warned by this incident, in which believable suggestions were being made by seemingly spiritual people using lots of religious language?

_____

_____

_____

INSPIRATION

Your heart is a fertile greenhouse ready to produce good fruit. Your mind is the doorway to your heart—the strategic place where you determine which seeds are sown and which seeds are discarded. The Holy Spirit is ready to help you manage and filter the thoughts that try to enter. He can help you guard your heart.

He stands with you on the threshold. A thought approaches, a questionable thought. Do you throw open the door and let it enter? Of course not. You *"fight to capture every thought until it acknowledges the authority of Christ"* (2 Corinthians 10:5 PHILLIPS). You don't leave the door unguarded. You stand equipped with handcuffs and leg irons, ready to capture any thought not fit to enter.

For the sake of discussion, let's say a thought regarding your personal value approaches. With all the cockiness of a neighborhood bully, the thought swaggers up to the door and says, "You're a loser. All your life you've been a loser. You've blown relationships and jobs and ambitions. You might as well write the word *bum* on your resume, for that is what you are."

The ordinary person would throw open the door and let the thought in. Like a seed from a weed, it would find fertile soil and take root and bear thorns of inferiority. The average person would say, "You're right. I'm a bum. Come on in."

But as a Christian, you aren't your average person. You are led by the Spirit. So rather than let the thought in, you take it captive. You handcuff it and march it down the street to the courthouse where you present the thought before the judgment seat of Christ.

"Jesus, this thought says I'm a bum and a loser and that I'll never amount to anything. What do you think?"

See what you are doing? You are submitting the thought to the authority of Jesus. If Jesus agrees with the thought, then let it in. If not, kick it out. In this case Jesus disagrees.

How do you know if Jesus agrees or disagrees? You open your Bible. (From *Just Like Jesus* by Max Lucado.)

REACTION

7. How would it change your life if you consistently developed this discipline of arresting and examining every thought?

_____

_____

_____

_____

8. What can you learn here in this passage about the character and resolve of your enemy?

_____

_____

_____

_____

_____

9. Why were Paul's ideas about how and what to think more valid than the ideas of the opposing religious leaders in Corinth?

_____

_____

_____

_____

_____

10. What concrete steps can you take to submit every thought to the authority of Christ (see Acts 17:10–12 for an example)?

_____

_____

_____

_____

_____

11. Can you think of a time when wrong thinking resulted in wrong choices in your life? How about when right thinking led to wise choices?

_____

_____

_____

12. What does this section of Paul's letter suggest about the role spiritual leaders play in helping their followers think and live in ways that honor God?

_____

_____

_____

_____

_____

_____

LIFE LESSONS

The universe is not a neutral place. There is a war taking place, and the primary battleground is in our minds. All day, every day, we are bombarded with words, ideas, images, and suggestions. From advertisements to blogs, and from scientists to TV preachers, we face continual exposure to various perspectives and values. Not all of the information to which we are exposed is true. Much of it is unhealthy and opposed to what God says. And since ideas always have consequences, and since what we believe ultimately does determine how we will behave, we must take radical action. What can we do? Wake up. Put on God's armor (see Ephesians 6). Pray for wisdom. Think critically. Practice discernment. Renew our minds daily.

DEVOTION

Almighty God, prompt us this day to remember that we are in a spiritual battle. What we think and believe will affect the way we live. Grant us the insight to see the world as you see it. Help us to think like Jesus more and more so that we live like him more and more.

JOURNALING

Think about the current state of your heart and mind. What are the thoughts that create the most havoc in your soul?

_____

_____

_____

_____

_____

_____

_____

_____

_____

_____

_____

_____

_____

_____

_____

_____

_____

_____

_____

_____

_____

_____

FOR FURTHER READING

To complete the book of 2 Corinthians during this twelve-part study, read 2 Corinthians 10:1–18. For more Bible passages on spiritual warfare, read Romans 13:12; 2 Corinthians 6:7; Ephesians 6:10–17; 1 Timothy 6:12; 1 Peter 2:11; and 5:8.

LESSON TEN

PERSEVERANCE

*Who is weak, and I do not feel weak? Who is led
into sin, and I do not inwardly burn? If I must boast,
I will boast of the things that show my weakness.*
2 CORINTHIANS 11:29–30

REFLECTION

In the Bible, the verb *persevere* literally means to "remain under." More than just the common notion of passively resigning to life's difficulties, the word suggests a courageous ability to bear hardships in a triumphant way. Given this meaning, who are your personal heroes of perseverance? Why do you look up to these individuals?

_____

_____

_____

_____

_____

SITUATION

Paul's critics had been making all kinds of foolish "boasts" about themselves in an effort to discredit his ministry. They had been preaching a message "other than the Jesus" that Paul and his coworkers had preached (see 2 Corinthians 11:4) and claimed that he was inferior to the original disciples (see verse 5). To refute these claims, Paul spells out a difference between him and them: if he were not a *genuine* apostle, called by God, then why would he willingly endure so much for the gospel? Why would he still be persevering in his work?

OBSERVATION

Read 2 Corinthians 11:16–31 from the New International Version or the New King James Version.

New International Version

16 I repeat: Let no one take me for a fool. But if you do, then tolerate me just as you would a fool, so that I may do a little boasting. 17 In this

self-confident boasting I am not talking as the Lord would, but as a fool. [18] Since many are boasting in the way the world does, I too will boast. [19] You gladly put up with fools since you are so wise! [20] In fact, you even put up with anyone who enslaves you or exploits you or takes advantage of you or puts on airs or slaps you in the face. [21] To my shame I admit that we were too weak for that!

Whatever anyone else dares to boast about—I am speaking as a fool—I also dare to boast about. [22] Are they Hebrews? So am I. Are they Israelites? So am I. Are they Abraham's descendants? So am I. [23] Are they servants of Christ? (I am out of my mind to talk like this.) I am more. I have worked much harder, been in prison more frequently, been flogged more severely, and been exposed to death again and again. [24] Five times I received from the Jews the forty lashes minus one. [25] Three times I was beaten with rods, once I was pelted with stones, three times I was shipwrecked, I spent a night and a day in the open sea, [26] I have been constantly on the move. I have been in danger from rivers, in danger from bandits, in danger from my fellow Jews, in danger from Gentiles; in danger in the city, in danger in the country, in danger at sea; and in danger from false believers. [27] I have labored and toiled and have often gone without sleep; I have known hunger and thirst and have often gone without food; I have been cold and naked. [28] Besides everything else, I face daily the pressure of my concern for all the churches. [29] Who is weak, and I do not feel weak? Who is led into sin, and I do not inwardly burn?

[30] If I must boast, I will boast of the things that show my weakness. [31] The God and Father of the Lord Jesus, who is to be praised forever, knows that I am not lying.

NEW KING JAMES VERSION

[16] I say again, let no one think me a fool. If otherwise, at least receive me as a fool, that I also may boast a little. [17] What I speak, I speak not according to the Lord, but as it were, foolishly, in this confidence of boasting. [18] Seeing that many boast according to the flesh, I also will boast. [19] For you put up with fools gladly, since you yourselves are wise!

[20] For you put up with it if one brings you into bondage, if one devours you, if one takes from you, if one exalts himself, if one strikes you on the face. [21] To our shame I say that we were too weak for that! But in whatever anyone is bold—I speak foolishly—I am bold also.

[22] Are they Hebrews? So am I. Are they Israelites? So am I. Are they the seed of Abraham? So am I. [23] Are they ministers of Christ?—I speak as a fool—I am more: in labors more abundant, in stripes above measure, in prisons more frequently, in deaths often. [24] From the Jews five times I received forty stripes minus one. [25] Three times I was beaten with rods; once I was stoned; three times I was shipwrecked; a night and a day I have been in the deep; [26] in journeys often, in perils of waters, in perils of robbers, in perils of my own countrymen, in perils of the Gentiles, in perils in the city, in perils in the wilderness, in perils in the sea, in perils among false brethren; [27] in weariness and toil, in sleeplessness often, in hunger and thirst, in fastings often, in cold and nakedness— [28] besides the other things, what comes upon me daily: my deep concern for all the churches. [29] Who is weak, and I am not weak? Who is made to stumble, and I do not burn with indignation?

[30] If I must boast, I will boast in the things which concern my infirmity. [31] The God and Father of our Lord Jesus Christ, who is blessed forever, knows that I am not lying.

EXPLORATION

1. When is it legitimate for a Christian to compare his or her "spiritual résumé" to another's?

_____

_____

_____

_____

_____

_____

2. According to Proverbs 27:2, you are to "let someone else praise you, and not your own mouth; an outsider, and not your own lips." How do you reconcile Paul's comments with the instruction given in this proverb?

_____

_____

_____

3. What is Paul actually "boasting" about in this passage? In what ways do his boasting represent an instruction to his readers on how to guard their minds?

_____

_____

_____

4. What is more difficult: enduring physical hardship or enduring emotional stress? Why?

_____

_____

5. What are some of the trials that Paul mentions? How do you think he was able to persevere in sharing the gospel in the midst of these crises?

_____

_____

_____

6. Why is perseverance such an important quality for Christian leaders today?

_____

_____

_____

INSPIRATION

One of God's cures for weak faith is a good, healthy struggle. Several years ago, our family visited Colonial Williamsburg, a re-creation of eighteenth-century America in Williamsburg, VA. If you ever visit there, pay special attention to the work of the silversmith. The craftsman places an ingot of silver on an anvil and pounds it with a sledgehammer. Once the metal is flat enough for shaping, into the furnace it goes. The worker alternately heats and pounds the metal until it takes the shape of a tool he can use.

Heating, pounding. Heating, pounding. Deadlines, traffic.

Arguments, disrespect. Loud sirens, silent phones.

Heating, pounding. Heating, pounding.

Did you know that the *smith* in *silversmith* comes from the old English word *smite*? Silversmiths are accomplished smiters. So is God. Once the worker is satisfied with the form of his tool, he begins to planish and pumice it. Using smaller hammers and abrasive pads, he taps, rubs, and decorates. And no one stops him. No one yanks the hammer out of his hand and says, "Go easy on that silver. You've pounded enough!" No, the craftsman buffets the metal until he is finished with it. Some silver-smiths, I'm told, keep polishing until they can see their face in the tool. When will God stop with you? When he sees his reflection in you. . . .

God guards those who turn to him. The pounding you feel does not suggest his distance, but proves his nearness. Trust his sovereignty. Hasn't he earned your trust? (From *Come Thirsty* by Max Lucado.)

REACTION

7. What do you think of this idea that God not only *allows* but often *participates* in the painful process of shaping of his children?

_____

_____

_____

8. What kinds of life situations are the most difficult for you to endure?

9. If critics attacked your character and faith, what "credentials" would you offer to show the genuineness of your Christian experience?

10. Do you agree with Paul's premise that perseverance is one of the defining marks of a believer in Christ? Why or why not?

11. How can you tell the difference between God-honoring perseverance and stubbornness or allegiance to a wrong cause?

12. What have been the greatest hardships in your life? What have you learned through them?

_____

_____

_____

_____

_____

_____

_____

_____

LIFE LESSONS

As imperfect people living among other flawed people in a fallen world, we should never be surprised when life is unpleasant. But more than that, we should recall that our status as children of God means the evil one singles us out for special attack. We can respond to these realities by complaining and becoming bitter. Or, we can decide—with divine help, and through the indwelling power of the Spirit of God—to endure triumphantly. We can let the irritations and trials of life shape us into the people God created us to be. When we surrender to the inevitable process, determined to hang in there and glorify Christ no matter what, our character changes. And as it does, we become powerful witnesses to the reality of God.

DEVOTION

Father, thank you for Paul's remarkable example—his rock-solid conviction of the reality of the gospel that enabled him to endure all kinds of difficulties. Make us willing to pay any price and bear any burden for the hope of making you smile and the joy of making you known.

JOURNALING

What are the most trying situations in your life at the present time for which you need a second wind of perseverance?

FOR FURTHER READING

To complete the book of 2 Corinthians during this twelve-part study, read 2 Corinthians 11:1–33. For more Bible passages on perseverance, read Romans 5:1–5; Galatians 6:9–10; Hebrews 10:32–36; 12:1–2; James 1:2–8; and Revelation 2:8–11.

LESSON ELEVEN

SUSTAINING GRACE

Therefore I take pleasure in infirmities, in reproaches, in needs, in persecutions, in distresses, for Christ's sake. For when I am weak, then I am strong.
2 CORINTHIANS 12:10 NKJV

REFLECTION

When people speak of their *testimony* or *spiritual journey*, they are referring to their unique personal experiences of responding to God's gracious involvement in their lives. In your own spiritual life, when and where have you encountered God most vividly?

_____

_____

_____

_____

_____

SITUATION

Paul has previously "boasted" about the work he has done among the Corinthians not to exalt himself or make himself seem more important to them, but to defend the truth of the gospel that he preached among them—a truth that his critics have openly challenged. In this next section of his letter, Paul will continue to "go on boasting"—but this time about his weaknesses in the form of an unknown "thorn in his side" that has caused him to learn how to rely on God's sustaining grace. Paul speaks candidly about all his experiences with God—certain sublime, ecstatic moments, but mostly long stretches of struggle.

OBSERVATION

Read 2 Corinthians 12:1–13 from the New International Version or the New King James Version.

New International Version

[1] I must go on boasting. Although there is nothing to be gained, I will go on to visions and revelations from the Lord. [2] I know a man in Christ

who fourteen years ago was caught up to the third heaven. Whether it was in the body or out of the body I do not know—God knows. ³ And I know that this man—whether in the body or apart from the body I do not know, but God knows— ⁴ was caught up to paradise and heard inexpressible things, things that no one is permitted to tell. ⁵ I will boast about a man like that, but I will not boast about myself, except about my weaknesses. ⁶ Even if I should choose to boast, I would not be a fool, because I would be speaking the truth. But I refrain, so no one will think more of me than is warranted by what I do or say, ⁷ or because of these surpassingly great revelations. Therefore, in order to keep me from becoming conceited, I was given a thorn in my flesh, a messenger of Satan, to torment me. ⁸ Three times I pleaded with the Lord to take it away from me. ⁹ But he said to me, "My grace is sufficient for you, for my power is made perfect in weakness." Therefore I will boast all the more gladly about my weaknesses, so that Christ's power may rest on me. ¹⁰ That is why, for Christ's sake, I delight in weaknesses, in insults, in hardships, in persecutions, in difficulties. For when I am weak, then I am strong.

¹¹ I have made a fool of myself, but you drove me to it. I ought to have been commended by you, for I am not in the least inferior to the "super-apostles," even though I am nothing. ¹² I persevered in demonstrating among you the marks of a true apostle, including signs, wonders and miracles. ¹³ How were you inferior to the other churches, except that I was never a burden to you? Forgive me this wrong!

NEW KING JAMES VERSION

¹ It is doubtless not profitable for me to boast. I will come to visions and revelations of the Lord: ² I know a man in Christ who fourteen years ago—whether in the body I do not know, or whether out of the body I do not know, God knows—such a one was caught up to the third heaven. ³ And I know such a man—whether in the body or out of the body I do not know, God knows— ⁴ how he was caught up into Paradise and heard inexpressible words, which it is not lawful for a man to utter.

⁵ Of such a one I will boast; yet of myself I will not boast, except in my infirmities. ⁶ For though I might desire to boast, I will not be a fool; for I will speak the truth. But I refrain, lest anyone should think of me above what he sees me to be or hears from me.

⁷ And lest I should be exalted above measure by the abundance of the revelations, a thorn in the flesh was given to me, a messenger of Satan to buffet me, lest I be exalted above measure. ⁸ Concerning this thing I pleaded with the Lord three times that it might depart from me. ⁹ And He said to me, "My grace is sufficient for you, for My strength is made perfect in weakness." Therefore most gladly I will rather boast in my infirmities, that the power of Christ may rest upon me. ¹⁰ Therefore I take pleasure in infirmities, in reproaches, in needs, in persecutions, in distresses, for Christ's sake. For when I am weak, then I am strong.

¹¹ I have become a fool in boasting; you have compelled me. For I ought to have been commended by you; for in nothing was I behind the most eminent apostles, though I am nothing. ¹² Truly the signs of an apostle were accomplished among you with all perseverance, in signs and wonders and mighty deeds. ¹³ For what is it in which you were inferior to other churches, except that I myself was not burdensome to you? Forgive me this wrong!

EXPLORATION

1. When Paul writes about "a man in Christ" who fourteen years ago had a vision, he is referring to his own experience. What exactly happened? What conclusion did Paul want his readers to draw from his story?

----

2. How did Paul use this experience to show that he was not inferior to other apostles?

_____

_____

_____

_____

3. What is Paul's struggle in choosing to tell this story and "boast" about himself? How does he seek to shift the focus off himself and on to God?

_____

_____

_____

_____

4. What do you think Paul means when he speaks of receiving a "thorn in the flesh"?

_____

_____

_____

_____

5. Why did Paul view this ongoing difficulty—whatever it was—as a good thing?

_____

_____

_____

6. How is Paul's attitude different from the more common "positive thinking"?

_____

_____

_____

INSPIRATION

You wonder why God doesn't remove temptation from your life? If he did, you might lean on your strength instead of his grace. A few stumbles might be what you need to convince you: His grace is sufficient for your sin.

You wonder why God doesn't remove the enemies in your life? Perhaps because he wants you to love like he loves. Anyone can love a friend, but only a few can love an enemy. So what if you aren't everyone's hero? His grace is sufficient for your self-image.

You wonder why God doesn't alter your personality? You, like Paul, are a bit rough around the edges? Say things you later regret or do things you later question? Why doesn't God make you more like him? He is. He's just not finished yet. Until he is, his grace is sufficient to overcome your flaws.

You wonder why God doesn't heal you? He *has* healed you. If you are in Christ, you have a perfected soul and a perfected body. His plan is to give you the soul now and the body when you get home. He may choose to heal parts of your body before heaven. But if he doesn't, don't you still have reason for gratitude? If he never gave you more than eternal life, could you ask for more than that? His grace is sufficient for gratitude.

Wonder why God won't give you a skill? If only God had made you a singer or a runner or a writer or a missionary. But there you are, tone-deaf, slow of foot and mind. Don't despair. God's grace is still sufficient to finish what he began. And until he's finished, let Paul remind you that the power is in the message, not the messenger. His grace is sufficient to speak clearly even when you don't.

For all we don't know about thorns, we can be sure of this. God would prefer we have an occasional limp than a perpetual strut. And if it takes a thorn for him to make his point, he loves us enough not to pluck it out.

God has every right to say no to us. We have every reason to say thanks to him. (From *In the Grip of Grace* by Max Lucado.)

REACTION

7. What would be your likely response if you had the strength and knowledge to handle every situation that came your way?

_____

_____

_____

8. Think of a recent situation in your life in which you found God's strength more than able to compensate for your personal inability. What did you learn from the experience?

_____

_____

_____

9. How can you tell when you are becoming spiritually proud?

_____

_____

_____

10. What are some of the ways God has humbled you in the past?

_____

_____

_____

11. How, practically speaking, can a Christian develop the quality of delighting in weakness and trusting more fully in the power of God?

_____

_____

12. Do you have a "thorn in the flesh" that God has not yet removed? If so, how do you think God has used it to make you stronger in your faith?

_____

_____

_____

_____

_____

_____

_____

_____

LIFE LESSONS

The Bible likens the Christian life to a lifelong walk or even a race (see 2 Timothy 4:7) down a narrow road (see Matthew 7:14). In other places, we find military metaphors to describe the Christian life (see Ephesians 6:10–17 and 2 Timothy 2:3–4). Such stark imagery—life as both a dangerous journey and a vicious battle—should prompt us to stop and ponder. How can we keep going to the end? How do we emerge victorious? Paul's experience and counsel are helpful. God does not protect his beloved children from trials. Rather, he helps us overcome them. Surprisingly, he works most effectively in and through our weaknesses. When we are clueless and powerless, we are much more likely to cry out to him and to cling to him. Whether times are good or bad, we live by grace. Always, we are called to rely fully on his amazing favor.

DEVOTION

How true it is, Lord, that you work and move in mysterious ways. Thank you for those moments when you are so near and real that we almost feel we can touch you. Thank you for the promise that in our darkest hours, you are with us and your grace is more than enough to sustain us.

JOURNALING

Where do you need to rely more on God's grace and power in your life?

FOR FURTHER READING

To complete the book of 2 Corinthians during this twelve-part study, read 2 Corinthians 12:1–13. For more Bible passages on strength in weakness, read 1 Samuel 17:1–58; Isaiah 40:28–31; Romans 8:26–30; 1 Corinthians 2:1–5; and Philippians 4:10–13.

LESSON TWELVE

SPIRITUAL MATURITY

Examine yourselves to see whether you are in the faith; test yourselves. Do you not realize that Christ Jesus is in you—unless, of course, you fail the test?
2 CORINTHIANS 13:5

REFLECTION

In the same way that every infant needs to grow up, each spiritual new-born also needs to mature in his or her faith. Three related questions: What does it look like to grow spiritually? How can a person tell if he or she is growing? When have you grown the most dramatically in your faith journey?

_____

_____

_____

_____

_____

_____

_____

_____

_____

_____

SITUATION

Throughout Paul's letter, he has defended his character, integrity, and work among the believers in Corinth in an effort to convince them of the truth of God's grace and love for them. He has recounted many of his trials and struggles to show the believers the sincerity of his heart and to encourage them to likewise persevere for the sake of the gospel. He has urged them to be wise and not be persuaded by false teachers and false doctrines. As he concludes his letter, he provides strong assurances of his love for them and again appeals for them to turn away from their worldly ways of thinking and living. In this manner, he provides the hallmarks of a healthy, mature Christian community: one filled with purity, humility, and unity.

OBSERVATION

*Read 2 Corinthians 12:19–13:11 from the New
International Version or the New King James Version.*

NEW INTERNATIONAL VERSION

¹²:¹⁹ Have you been thinking all along that we have been defending ourselves to you? We have been speaking in the sight of God as those in Christ; and everything we do, dear friends, is for your strengthening. ²⁰ For I am afraid that when I come I may not find you as I want you to be, and you may not find me as you want me to be. I fear that there may be discord, jealousy, fits of rage, selfish ambition, slander, gossip, arrogance and disorder. ²¹ I am afraid that when I come again my God will humble me before you, and I will be grieved over many who have sinned earlier and have not repented of the impurity, sexual sin and debauchery in which they have indulged.

¹³:¹ This will be my third visit to you. "Every matter must be established by the testimony of two or three witnesses." ² I already gave you a warning when I was with you the second time. I now repeat it while absent: On my return I will not spare those who sinned earlier or any of the others, ³ since you are demanding proof that Christ is speaking through me. He is not weak in dealing with you, but is powerful among you. ⁴ For to be sure, he was crucified in weakness, yet he lives by God's power. Likewise, we are weak in him, yet by God's power we will live with him in our dealing with you.

⁵ Examine yourselves to see whether you are in the faith; test yourselves. Do you not realize that Christ Jesus is in you—unless, of course, you fail the test? ⁶ And I trust that you will discover that we have not failed the test. ⁷ Now we pray to God that you will not do anything wrong—not so that people will see that we have stood the test but so that you will do what is right even though we may seem to have failed. ⁸ For we cannot do anything against the truth, but only for the truth. ⁹ We are glad whenever we are weak but you are strong; and our prayer is that you may be fully

restored. [10] This is why I write these things when I am absent, that when I come I may not have to be harsh in my use of authority—the authority the Lord gave me for building you up, not for tearing you down.

[11] Finally, brothers and sisters, rejoice! Strive for full restoration, encourage one another, be of one mind, live in peace. And the God of love and peace will be with you.

New King James Version

[12:19] Again, do you think that we excuse ourselves to you? We speak before God in Christ. But we do all things, beloved, for your edification. [20] For I fear lest, when I come, I shall not find you such as I wish, and that I shall be found by you such as you do not wish; lest there be contentions, jealousies, outbursts of wrath, selfish ambitions, back-bitings, whisperings, conceits, tumults; [21] lest, when I come again, my God will humble me among you, and I shall mourn for many who have sinned before and have not repented of the uncleanness, fornication, and lewdness which they have practiced.

[13:1] This will be the third time I am coming to you. "By the mouth of two or three witnesses every word shall be established." [2] I have told you before, and foretell as if I were present the second time, and now being absent I write to those who have sinned before, and to all the rest, that if I come again I will not spare— [3] since you seek a proof of Christ speaking in me, who is not weak toward you, but mighty in you. [4] For though He was crucified in weakness, yet He lives by the power of God. For we also are weak in Him, but we shall live with Him by the power of God toward you.

[5] Examine yourselves as to whether you are in the faith. Test yourselves. Do you not know yourselves, that Jesus Christ is in you?—unless indeed you are disqualified. [6] But I trust that you will know that we are not disqualified.

[7] Now I pray to God that you do no evil, not that we should appear approved, but that you should do what is honorable, though we may seem disqualified. [8] For we can do nothing against the truth, but for the

truth. ⁹ For we are glad when we are weak and you are strong. And this also we pray, that you may be made complete. ¹⁰ Therefore I write these things being absent, lest being present I should use sharpness, according to the authority which the Lord has given me for edification and not for destruction.

¹¹ Finally, brethren, farewell. Become complete. Be of good comfort, be of one mind, live in peace; and the God of love and peace will be with you.

EXPLORATION

1. Paul has made a number of statements in this letter to defending his work and ministry. What does he say is the reason for why he gave this defense?

_____

_____

_____

2. Paul lists some negative behaviors he fears are still persistent among the Corinthians. How would his list differ if he were writing to your church or small group?

_____

_____

_____

3. What does Paul mean by living "by God's power" (2 Corinthians 13:4)? What does this look like in your everyday life?

_____

_____

_____

4. What does it mean to "examine yourselves to see whether you are in the faith" (verse 5)? Why do you think this is necessary for believers in Christ to do?

_____

_____

_____

5. Despite Paul's stern words, his desire was to build up the Corinthians, not tear them down (see verse 10). What are some specific ways Christians can build up one another?

_____

_____

_____

6. In closing, Paul pleads with his readers to "strive for full restoration, encourage one another, be of one mind, live in peace" (verse 11). Why is this so much more easily said than done?

_____

_____

_____

INSPIRATION

Suspicion and distrust often lurk at God's table. The Baptists distrust the Methodists. The Church of Christ avoids the Presbyterians. The Calvinists scoff at the Armenians. Charismatics. Immersionists. Patternists. Around the table the siblings squabble, and the Father sighs.

The Father sighs because he has a dream. "I have other sheep that are not of this sheep pen. I must bring them also. They too will listen to my voice, and there shall be one flock and one shepherd" (John 10:16).

God has only one flock. Somehow we missed that. Religious division is not his idea. Franchises and sectarianism are not in God's plan.

God has one flock. The flock has one shepherd. And though we may think there are many, we are wrong. There is only one.

Never in the Bible are we told to create unity. We are simply told to maintain the unity that exists. Paul exhorts us to "make every effort to keep the unity of the Spirit through the bond of peace" (Ephesians 4:3). Our task is not to invent unity, but to acknowledge it . . .

By the way, the church names we banter about? They do not exist in heaven. The Book of Life does not list your denomination next to your name. Why? Because it is not the denomination that saves you. And I wonder, if there are no denominations in heaven, why do we have denominations on earth?

What would happen (I know this is a crazy thought), but what would happen if all the churches agreed, on a given day, to change their names to simply "church"? What if any reference to any denomination were removed and we were all just Christians? And then when people chose which church to attend, they wouldn't do so by the sign outside . . . they'd do so by the hearts of the people inside. And then when people were asked what church they attended, their answer wouldn't be a label but just a location.

And then we Christians wouldn't be known for what divides us; instead we'd be known for what unites us—our common Father. Crazy idea? Perhaps.

But I think God would like it. It was his to begin with. (From *A Gentle Thunder* by Max Lucado.)

REACTION

7. How can you, like Paul, develop the courageous willingness to speak frankly but lovingly to others about the importance of growing spiritually?

_____

_____

_____

_____

8. Is it a common practice for you to take a "spiritual inventory"? How, and how often, should one do such a thing?

_____

_____

_____

_____

9. What people in your life need to be built up today, and in what ways?

_____

_____

_____

_____

10. What does it mean, in practical terms, to "become complete" (2 Corinthians 13:11 NKJV)?

_____

_____

_____

_____

11. Do you currently have relationships with other believers marked by friction and discord? If so, what do you feel God urging you to do?

_____

_____

_____

_____

12. As you think back over this study, what primary lessons or principles have meant the most to you? Why do those lessons stand out to you?

_____

_____

_____

_____

LIFE LESSONS

It is the nature of healthy organisms to grow. The failure of a living thing to mature and thrive is not normal. A child who develops slowly, or not at all, is a cause of great concern. Appointments are made. Specialists are consulted. Tests are conducted. In the same way, those who know Christ should be developing spiritually. There should be some signs of growth and change. When we claim to be followers of Christ, but we do not exhibit the conduct and character of Christ, something is clearly wrong. So examine your own life. Do you have a desire for personal purity? Are you marked by a growing humility? Do you pursue unity with other believers? These are reliable indicators of divine transformation.

DEVOTION

Father, we are reminded again that not growing is not an option for your children. You have begun a good work in us that will continue until Christ comes again. Make us a willing partner in this great eternal makeover. Thank you for your patience when we stumble.

JOURNALING

What are two or three areas of your life in which you would like God to help you mature?

_____

_____

_____

_____

_____

_____

_____

FOR FURTHER READING

To complete the book of 2 Corinthians during this twelve-part study, read 2 Corinthians 12:14–13:14. For more Bible passages on maturity, read 1 Corinthians 3:1–4; Ephesians 4:14–15; Philippians 1:3–6; Hebrews 6:1–3; and 1 Peter 2:1–3.

LEADER'S GUIDE FOR SMALL GROUPS

Thank you for your willingness to lead a group through *Life Lessons from 2 Corinthians*. The rewards of being a leader are different from those of participating, and we hope you find your own walk with Jesus deepened by this experience. During the twelve lessons in this study, you will guide your group through selected passages in 2 Corinthians and explore the key themes of the letter. There are several elements in this leader's guide that will help you as you structure your study and reflection time, so be sure to follow along and take advantage of each one.

BEFORE YOU BEGIN

Before your first meeting, make sure the group members have their own copy of the *Life Lessons from 2 Corinthians.* study guide so they can follow along and have their answers written out ahead of time. Alternately, you can hand out the guides at your first meeting and give the group some time to look over the material and ask any preliminary questions. Be sure to send a sheet around the room during that first meeting and have the members write down their name, phone number, and email address so you can keep in touch with them during the week.

There are several ways to structure the duration of the study. You can choose to cover each lesson individually for a total of twelve weeks of discussion, or you can combine two lessons together per week for a total of six weeks of discussion. You can also choose to have the group members read just the selected passages of Scripture given in each lesson, or they can cover the entire book of 2 Corinthians by reading the material listed in the "For Further Reading" section at the end of each lesson. The following table illustrates these options:

Twelve-Week Format

Week	Lessons Covered	Simplified Reading	Expanded Reading
1	Suffering	2 Corinthians 1:1–11	2 Corinthians 1:1–11
2	Planning and Integrity	2 Corinthians 1:12–2:4	2 Corinthians 1:12–2:13
3	God's New Agreement	2 Corinthians 3:4–18	2 Corinthians 2:14–3:18
4	Shining the Light	2 Corinthians 4:1–15	2 Corinthians 4:1–15
5	Eternal Perspective	2 Corinthians 4:16–5:10	2 Corinthians 4:16–5:21
6	Living as a Servant	2 Corinthians 6:1–10	2 Corinthians 6:1–7:1
7	Follow the Leader	2 Corinthians 7:2–16	2 Corinthians 7:2–16
8	Money Matters	2 Corinthians 9:1–15	2 Corinthians 8:1–9:15
9	Ground Zero	2 Corinthians 10:1–18	2 Corinthians 10:1–18
10	Perseverance	2 Corinthians 11:16–31	2 Corinthians 11:1–33
11	Sustaining Grace	2 Corinthians 12:1–13	2 Corinthians 12:1–13
12	Spiritual Maturity	2 Corinthians 12:19–13:11	2 Corinthians 12:14–13:14

Six-Week Format

Week	Lessons Covered	Simplified Reading	Expanded Reading
1	Suffering / Planning and Integrity	2 Corinthians 1:1–2:4	2 Corinthians 1:1–2:13
2	God's New Agreement / Shining the Light	2 Corinthians 3:3–4:15	2 Corinthians 2:14–4:15
3	Eternal Perspective / Living as a Servant	2 Corinthians 4:16–5:10; 6:1–10	2 Corinthians 4:16–7:1
4	Follow the Leader / Money Matters	2 Corinthians 7:2–16; 9:1–15	2 Corinthians 7:2–9:15

Week	Lessons Covered	Simplified Reading	Expanded Reading
5	Ground Zero / Perseverance	2 Corinthians 10:1–18; 11:16–31	2 Corinthians 10:1–11:33
6	Sustaining Grace / Spiritual Maturity	2 Corinthians 12:1–13; 12:19–13:11	2 Corinthians 12:1–13:14

Generally, the ideal size you will want for the group is between eight to ten people, which ensures everyone will have enough time to participate in discussions. If you have more people, you might want to break up the main group into smaller subgroups. Encourage those who show up at the first meeting to commit to attending the duration of the study, as this will help the group members get to know each other, create stability for the group, and help you know how to prepare each week.

Each of the lessons begins with a brief reflection that highlights the theme you will be discussing that week. As you begin your group time, have the group members briefly respond to the opening question to get them thinking about the topic at hand. Some people may want to tell a long story in response to one of these questions, but the goal is to keep the answers brief. Ideally, you want everyone in the group to get a chance to answer, so try to keep the responses to just a few minutes. If you have more talkative group members, say up front that everyone needs to limit his or her answer to two minutes.

Give the group members a chance to answer, but tell them to feel free to pass if they wish. With the rest of the study, it's generally not a good idea to have everyone answer every question—a free-flowing discussion is more desirable. But with the opening reflection question, you can go around the circle. Encourage shy people to share, but don't force them.

Before your first meeting, let the group members know how the lessons are broken down. During your group discussion time the members will be drawing on the answers they wrote to the Exploration and Reaction sections, so encourage them to always complete these ahead of time. Also, invite them to bring any questions and insights they uncovered while reading to your next meeting, especially if they had a breakthrough moment or if they didn't understand something they read.

WEEKLY PREPARATION

As the leader, there are a few things you should do to prepare for each meeting:

- *Read through the lesson.* This will help you to become familiar with the content and know how to structure the discussion times.
- *Decide which questions you want to discuss.* Depending on how you structure your group time, you may not be able to cover every question. So select the questions ahead of time that you absolutely want the group to explore.
- *Be familiar with the questions you want to discuss.* When the group meets you'll be watching the clock, so you want to make sure you are familiar with the Bible study questions you have selected. You can then spend time in the passage again when the group meets. In this way, you'll ensure you have the passage more deeply in your mind than your group members.
- *Pray for your group.* Pray for your group members throughout the week and ask God to lead them as they study his Word.
- *Bring extra supplies to your meeting.* The members should bring their own pens for writing notes, but it's a good idea to have extras available for those who forget. You may also want to bring paper and additional Bibles.

Note that in many cases there will not be one "right" answer to the question. Answers will vary, especially when the group members are being asked to share their personal experiences.

STRUCTURING THE DISCUSSION TIME

You will need to determine with your group how long you want to meet each week so you can plan your time accordingly. Generally, most groups like to meet for either sixty minutes or ninety minutes, so you could use one of the following schedules:

Section	60 Minutes	90 Minutes
WELCOME (members arrive and get settled)	5 minutes	10 minutes
REFLECTION (discuss the opening question for the lesson)	10 minutes	15 minutes
DISCUSSION (discuss the Bible study questions in the Exploration and Reaction sections)	35 minutes	50 minutes
PRAYER/CLOSING (pray together as a group and dismiss)	10 minutes	15 minutes

As the group leader, it is up to you to keep track of the time and keep things moving along according to your schedule. You might want to set a timer for each segment so both you and the group members know when your time is up. (Note that there are some good phone apps for timers that play a gentle chime or other pleasant sound instead of a disruptive noise.) Don't feel pressured to cover every question you have selected if the group has a good discussion going. Again, it's not necessary to go around the circle and make everyone share.

Don't be concerned if the group members are silent or slow to share. People are often quiet when they are pulling together their ideas, and this might be a new experience for them. Just ask a question and let it hang in the air until someone shares. You can then say, "Thank you. What about others? What came to you when you reflected on the passage?"

GROUP DYNAMICS

Leading a group through *Life Lessons from 2 Corinthians* will prove to be highly rewarding both to you and your group members—but that doesn't mean you will not encounter any challenges along the way! Discussions can get off track. Group members may not be sensitive to the needs and ideas of others. Some might worry they will be expected to talk about matters that make them feel awkward. Others may express comments that result in disagreements. To help ease this strain on you and the group, consider the following ground rules:

- When someone raises a question or comment that is off the main topic, suggest you deal with it another time, or, if you feel led to go in that direction, let the group know you will be spending some time discussing it.
- If someone asks a question you don't know how to answer, admit it and move on. At your discretion, feel free to invite group members to comment on questions that call for personal experience.
- If you find one or two people are dominating the discussion time, direct a few questions to others in the group. Outside the main group time, ask the more dominating members to help you draw out the quieter ones. Work to make them a part of the solution instead of the problem.
- When a disagreement occurs, encourage the group members to process the matter in love. Encourage those on opposite sides to restate what they heard the other side say about the matter, and then invite each side to evaluate if that perception is accurate. Lead the group in examining other Scriptures related to the topic and look for common ground.

When any of these issues arise, encourage your group members to follow the words from the Bible: "Love one another" (John 13:34), "If it is possible, as far as it depends on you, live at peace with everyone" (Romans 12:18), and, "Be quick to listen, slow to speak and slow to become angry" (James 1:19).

Thank you again for taking the time to lead your group. May God reward your efforts and dedication and make your time together in this study fruitful for his kingdom.

ALSO AVAILABLE IN THE LIFE LESSONS SERIES

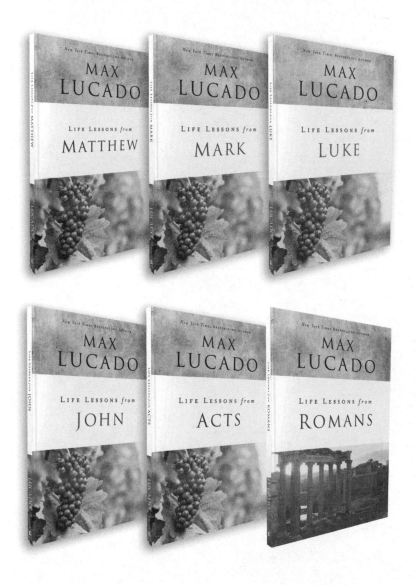

Now available wherever books and ebooks are sold.